SYDNEY

50 magic moments

ABOUT THE AUTHORS

Andrew Conway is a travel writer and TV columnist. Born in London, he worked on local and provincial newspapers in the UK before migrating to Sydney in 1985. He worked for *The Australian* and *The Sun-Herald* as a news reporter and was travel editor of *The Sun-Herald* and *The Sydney Morning Herald* for six years before setting up his own freelance agency. He and his wife, Sue Bennett, live in Sydney.

Sue Bennett is food and wine editor of *The Daily Telegraph*. She has been a journalist all her working life, including three years as editor of *The North Shore Times*, a Sydney regional newspaper. She was born in Manchester and migrated to Australia in 1985.

Introduction

The idea for this book came while sitting on the back of the Manly ferry as it sailed across Sydney Harbour. It was one of those perfect autumn days when the sun was warm, the air crisp and fresh, the sky clear and cloudless.

The city and harbour looked magnificent. The sails of the Opera House glinted in the sunlight, backed by the towering arch of the Harbour Bridge. The harbour was awash with yachts, their spinnakers billowing and flapping in the breeze.

Great swathes of bushland and slivers of beaches filled the horizon as we sailed past the rugged Sydney Heads. The view was breathtakingly beautiful – in short, one of life's magic moments.

Sydney, and the surrounding countryside of the Blue Mountains, Hunter Valley and South Coast, are brimming with magic moments just like this. The question is, where do you find them?

Look no further. 50 Magic Moments is your personal guide to one of the world's most beautiful and exciting cities.

In this easy-to-read guide book, we've listed the 50 best places to explore, discover and enjoy in the biggest and most vibrant city in Australia, the home of the 2000 Olympic and Paralympic Games.

Whether you live in Sydney or are visiting for the first time, this is the only guide you'll need to enjoy the city's finest attractions and savour a quintessential slice of Sydney life.

With each attraction, we've included simple directions from Circular Quay – the city's main harbour ferry hub and a centre for buses, trains and taxis – as well as prices, opening times, telephone numbers and website addresses where available.

We've also included a detailed list of what we consider to be the city's best hotels and restaurants, as well as a host of other attractions to help you get the most out of your time in Sydney.

And our 50 magic moments? Well, they're 50 special highlights, one at each attraction, which we believe will provide you with treasured memories of your visit.

This book is not a definitive guide to the city and surrounds – we're certain you'll find your own special places. This is simply our selection of the best sights in Sydney, and a few places beyond the city, which we hope will fill your visit with a swag of magic moments.

50 Magic Moments

● **magic**moment locations

Sydney Snapshot

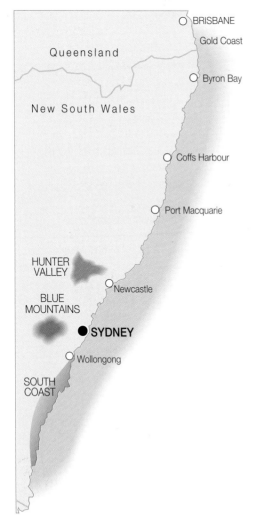

Sydney is the largest city in Australia, with a population of four million, and the capital of New South Wales, Australia's most populous State. It's also a major financial and trading centre for the Asia-Pacific region.

Greater Sydney is one of the world's largest cities, stretching 80 kilometres north to south, 70 kilometres east to west, a sprawling mass of red-roofed suburbs, bushland, rivers, beaches, bays, lakes, commercial and industrial centres.

Sydney has a temperate climate. The seasons are: Summer, December-February; Autumn, March-May; Winter, June-August; Spring, September-November. The average temperature is 22° Celsius in summer, 13° Celsius in winter. Sydney boasts an average 342 days of sunshine a year; the average annual rainfall is 1216mm, heaviest between February and July.

Aborigines lived in the Sydney region for at least 40,000 years before European settlement.

Captain James Cook first set foot in New South Wales at Botany Bay on April 29, 1770, claiming it as a colony of the British Empire.

The First Fleet sailed into Port Jackson (Sydney Harbour) under the command of Captain Arthur Phillip on January 26, 1788. The first colonial settlement at Sydney Cove was founded the following day.

New South Wales became a state of the Australian nation at Federation on January 1, 1901.

Sydney hosts the 2000 Olympic Games from Friday, September 15 to Sunday, October 1, and the 2000 Paralympic Games from Wednesday, October 18 to Sunday, October 29.

Telephone numbers are for calls made within Sydney. If you're calling from outside Sydney but within Australia, the prefix is 02. For international calls, the prefix is: 61 2 followed by the number.
Admission prices quoted are for adults only, except where the attraction is family oriented. Entry fees for children, concessions and family passes are available at most Sydney attractions.

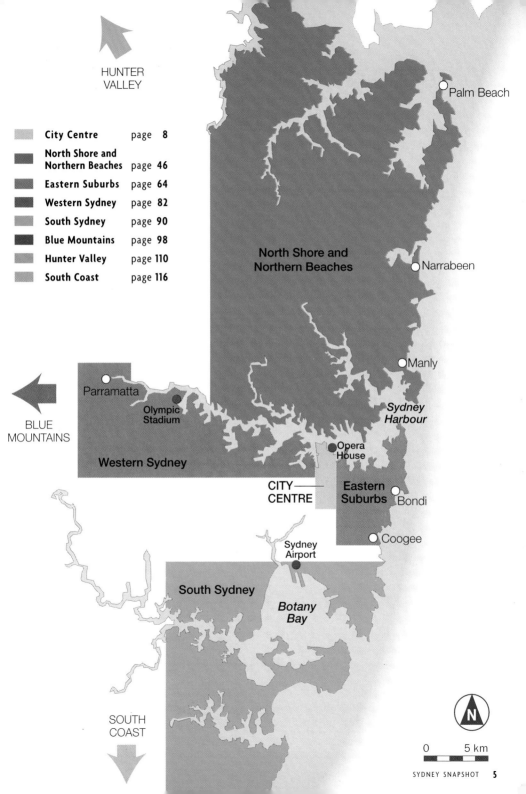

HUNTER
VALLEY

Palm Beach

North Shore and
Northern Beaches

Narrabeen

Manly

Sydney
Harbour

BLUE
MOUNTAINS

Parramatta

Olympic
Stadium

Western Sydney

Opera
House

CITY
CENTRE

Eastern
Suburbs

Bondi

Coogee

Sydney
Airport

South Sydney

Botany
Bay

SOUTH
COAST

N

0   5 km

Welcome to Sydney

It was Captain Arthur Phillip, commander of the First Fleet, who gave Sydney its first tourist accolade. "We got into Port Jackson early in the afternoon," he wrote in his ship's journal on January 26, 1788, "and had the satisfaction of finding the finest harbour in the world." Two hundred years on, his words still ring true.

The ancient landscape may have been covered with modern skyscrapers and the Aboriginal tribespeople replaced by a melting pot of cultures from around the world. The population may have grown from the original convict settlement of 1,044 unfortunates to more than four million fortunates, and the old masted sailing ships overtaken by sleek yachts and high-speed catamarans, but the sun still shines down on the world's most beautiful harbour.

How many times have Phillip's words been repeated by generations of new arrivals, immigrants and tourists alike, who are captivated by the sheer natural beauty of this extraordinary city? It's a jaded traveller indeed who arrives on one of those cloudless days, when the sun shimmers on the white-tiled roof of the Sydney Opera House and sparkles on the water of the harbour, and fails to be moved by its abundant charm.

Founded by convict labour, built on the blood, sweat and tears of pioneers, moulded by a multicultural population with an uncommon vision and strength of character, and forged into a modern, vibrant and spirited community, Sydney is a city of – and for – the new millennium.

Little wonder, then, that it was chosen to host the 2000 Olympic and Paralympic Games. Like a float being prepared for a carnival, the city has undergone the biggest and most ambitious civic improvement program in a century, a $6.5 billion facelift in preparation for the world's biggest sporting event.

New hotels, restaurants and cafes are opening by the week. Major public attractions are being restored, repaired and improved. Pavements have been widened,

the international and domestic airports upgraded, and shops given the new millennium touch-up. All of which means this is an exciting time to be visiting Sydney.

To many people, Sydney is the Opera House, Harbour Bridge and harbour but the city extends far beyond these three world-famous icons.

One of the surprises of Sydney is its "greenness", with vast swathes of the harbour and surrounding suburbs covered with thick bushland, exquisite plants and wildflowers, colourful birds and native wildlife from ring-tailed possums to fruit bats.

Much of the harbour foreshore is dedicated national park and two others, Ku-ring-gai Chase to the north and the Royal National Park to the south, are classic Australian bushland at its best.

Another feature which takes visitors by surprise is Sydney's "openness", a relaxed and informal atmosphere, fostered by a breezy outdoor lifestyle, which permeates the city.

Sydneysiders, as they are known, work hard and play hard. They'll climb the economic coal-face five days a week but they'll surf, swim and rollerblade back

down it at weekends. They'll work long hours at the office but know that the good life is right outside. The temperate climate, combined with the city's beautiful harbour, beaches and parks, offers a lifestyle that's almost too good to be true – almost.

Sydney's obsession with health and exercise means you'll see almost as many joggers pounding the city streets and parks as sharp-suited office workers. Its love affair with good food and wine extends from five-star restaurants to beachside barbecues. Its passion for sport is all-consuming.

Sydney is hedonism personified. Unlike Melbourne, its more refined southern cousin, Sydney likes to show off, and why not? The city has the best beaches, restaurants, cafes, tourist attractions, sporting venues, hotels, and theatres in Australia – or so it says.

One thing is certain. The city's melting pot of nationalities, fuelled by the ongoing arrival of immigrants from around the world, lends Sydney a multicultural character matched by few other cities.

Nowhere is this more obvious than the variety of ethnic restaurants and cafes throughout the city.

Sydney is far from perfect. Like any major city, crime, pollution, drugs and graffiti are all too common problems. Much of the city's rich architectural history has been lost forever, swamped by the tide of modern development, and Sydney's Aboriginal heritage has largely disappeared from the cultural landscape. It still exists in certain museums, galleries, shops and scattered rock art sites but you'll have to search for it.

On the upside, Sydney is a safe, friendly, exciting and beautiful city. It has an extensive public transport system and many natural attractions, like the wonderful beaches and parks, are free.

In summer, it's hot and humid, winter can be surprisingly cold, and when it rains, it pours down in buckets but for the most part Sydney basks in glorious sunshine under a deep blue sky.

Good food, fine wine, friendly people, and the sort of attractions that most countries would sell their souls for, all in one beautiful city. What more could you possibly want?

The city skyline from Bradfield Park, Kirribilli.

Opera House

1

magicmoment

Standing in the northern foyer bars of the Opera Theatre or Concert Hall, during interval in an evening performance, with the lights of the Harbour Bridge and harbour all around you. Champagne optional.

mustsee

A performance in the Concert Hall or Opera Theatre with their soaring vaulted ceilings.

mustdo

One of the daily front-of-house tours, $12.90 (see Directions); there are also occasional backstage tours, $20.90. NB: Both involve many steps; tours for disabled people can be arranged.

The story of the Sydney Opera House is worthy of a dramatic opera itself.

Act one: The visionary Danish architect Joern Utzon wins an international prize in 1957 to design a new performing arts centre. His plan features a daring yet breathtaking building of vaulted shells, covered in white tiles and spread like sails above a pink granite podium straddling Bennelong Point.

Act two: The design and construction are fraught with problems. The costs soar, political debate rages, the public becomes anxious, and intrigue and in-fighting of Machiavellian proportions ensue. The first blood is spilled. An angry and frustrated Utzon says he can no longer work to the political demands, resigns in 1966, and leaves Australia.

Act three: A new team of architects completes the exterior and redesigns the interior. An Opera House lottery raises $100 million to cover the budget blow-out. Utzon's dream, forecast to cost $7 million and take four years to complete, finally costs $102 million and spans 16 years.

What could so easily have been a Greek tragedy of epic proportions has a happy ending. On October 20, 1973, a million people line the harbour foreshores to see Queen Elizabeth II officially declare the building open. Cheers and applause all round.

A quarter of a century later, the Sydney Opera House remains a wonder of the modern era, one of the world's most recognisable buildings, a unique Australian icon, a magnificent performance space, and a source of great public pride.

Perched in the box seat of Sydney Harbour, and framed by the city skyscrapers and soaring arch of the Harbour Bridge, the Opera House appears to float like a tall ship, its white sails billowing in the breeze. Almost a piece of modern sculpture than a performing arts centre, it is, not surprisingly, the most visited, photographed and admired tourist attraction in Australia.

To appreciate the scale and purpose of the Opera House, you need to do a guided tour. The shells, covered by more than a million individual tiles made in Sweden, conceal five performance spaces: a 2,679-seat concert hall, a 1,547-seat opera theatre, a 544-seat drama theatre, 398-seat playhouse and studio, offering music, opera, drama, ballet, dance and concerts throughout the year.

The building contains five rehearsal rooms, 60 dressing rooms, the five-star Bennelong restaurant, a cafe, several bars, administration offices, gift shops and two restaurants. It's also the venue for a decent Sunday craft market.

The best exterior views are from the Monumental Steps, modelled by Utzon on the Mayan temples of Mexico, and the northern and western broadwalks which lead around the Opera House to provide panoramic views of the harbour.

Directions You can walk to the Opera House from the east side of Circular Quay. By car, approach from Macquarie Street; there's an underground car park. There are daily guided front-of-house tours (9250 7250), 9.15am-4pm (except Good Friday and Christmas Day), $12.90 adult. Box office bookings (9250 7777); www.soh.nsw.gov.au

The Sydney Opera House in full sail.

Harbour Bridge

2

magicmoment

Walking over the arch of the Harbour Bridge with BridgeClimb Sydney (see Directions). There are 1,337 steps to negotiate and you'll need a good head for heights but the view from the top is exhilarating.

mustsee

The museum in the south-eastern pylon, dedicated to the building of the bridge.

mustdo

Climb up to the viewing platform on top of the south-eastern pylon (see Directions). You'll have to climb 200 steps but the city and harbour views are spectacular.

There are two certainties about Sydney. The Opera House would be nothing without the harbour and the harbour would be nothing without its bridge. Put the three elements together and you have the backdrop for one of the world's most beautiful cities.

Spanning the harbour like a giant coathanger, the Harbour Bridge is to Sydney what Tower Bridge is to London and the Golden Gate Bridge is to San Francisco. It's not just a bridge, it's part of the fabric of Sydney, a national icon anchored at the heart of the city's identity.

It's all but impossible to look at the bridge without a sense of awe. From the tip of its arch to the toes of its granite pylons, one of the world's longest and heaviest single-arch span bridges is a sight to behold.

The statistics speak for themselves: completed in 1932, after eight years of blood, sweat and toil, the bridge stretches for 1,149 metres, the arch alone extending almost half that distance. There are 52,800 tonnes of steel, held together by six million rivets

and covered with 80,000 litres of steel-grey paint.

It carries two rail tracks, eight lanes of highway, a bicycle track and pedestrian walkway, and hundreds of thousands of people as they cross each day between the north and south of the city.

Civic leaders had been planning a harbour bridge, linking Milsons Point to the north and Dawes Point to the south, for almost a century before construction began in 1924.

The bridge became one of the engineering feats of its time, continuing through the Great Depression of the 1920s and creating much-needed jobs. Fourteen hundred workers toiled on the structure; 16 lost their lives.

The opening ceremony, on March 19, 1932, was a spectacle in itself. Just as the NSW Premier, Jack Lang, was about to cut the official ribbon, a zealous royalist, Captain Francis de Groot, galloped forward and slashed the ribbon with his sword in the name of King, Empire and "the decent citizens of New South Wales".

De Groot was arrested (and later fined five pounds), the ribbon was hastily tied back together, and the bridge opened to headlines around the world proclaiming it to be "one of the seven wonders of the modern world".

If you want to see the bridge close up, the best way is to walk across it from The Rocks or Milsons Point on the north shore. The pedestrian walkway offers magnificent views of the harbour and city, and while the wire fence is to stop people leaping off, there are plenty of gaps for photographs.

You can climb into the south-eastern pylon (the one closest to the city) which has a museum, dedicated to the building of the bridge, and an open-air viewing platform.

BridgeClimb Sydney offers walks over the arch of the bridge providing spectacular views of the harbour and city. You have to wear a protective overall and harness attached to the bridge railings, and you'll need a good head for heights, but the climb is an amazing experience.

The four-lane Sydney Harbour Tunnel, opened in 1996, has relieved some of its load but the Harbour Bridge remains a vital artery for Sydney traffic and a monument to human ingenuity.

Directions Walk onto the Harbour Bridge via steps in Cumberland Street at The Rocks or near Milsons Point train station in Kirribilli. The south-east pylon is open daily, 10am-5pm (except Christmas Day), $2 entry from the pedestrian walkway (9247 3408). BridgeClimb Sydney costs from $98 adult, bookings essential (9252 0077); www.bridgeclimb.com

... and night.

The Harbour

3

magicmoment

Cruising Sydney Harbour under a cloudless sky, with the sun sparkling on the water and the sails of yachts billowing in the breeze.

mustsee

The beaches, bays, inlets, bushland and million-dollar homes lining the harbour foreshores. The foreshore is also dotted with ancient Aboriginal sites which can be viewed on certain walks and tours (see page 134).

mustdo

A harbour cruise (see Directions).

Sydneysiders have an almost spiritual attachment to their harbour and it's not hard to see why. One look at this expanse of sparkling water, arguably the most beautiful urban setting in the world, is enough to convince most people that Sydney has been blessed by nature.

Sydney Harbour, or Port Jackson as it's officially known, has managed to survive the ravages of 200 years of urban explosion and emerge more captivating as each year goes by.

Bounded by 240 kilometres of bays, inlets, beaches and bushland, dotted with five islands – Shark, Clark, Fort Denison, Goat and Rodd – and backed by a towering city skyline, the harbour is the undisputed jewel in Sydney's crown.

If you're fortunate enough to have a window seat as your plane lands at Sydney Airport, or a harbour-view room in a high-rise hotel, your first sight of the harbour is little short of breathtaking but the best way to enjoy it is on the water.

A harbour cruise should be one of your first excursions, not only to get your bearings but to see the city in all its glory. A range of cruises departs throughout the day from Circular Quay (see page 134).

Sydney Harbour is actually made up of three distinct elements: the deep-water main harbour leading out through the rugged North and South Heads into the Pacific Ocean; Middle Harbour, a bush-covered expanse of bays, beaches and inlets; and the Parramatta River to the west of the Harbour Bridge.

It's the main harbour which is the focal point, awash with ferries, tankers, tugs, cargo ships, prawn trawlers, naval vessels, liners, water taxis, fishing boats, the occasional seaplane, and the billowing sails of private yachts, all combining work and play with seamless ease.

This is perhaps what makes Sydney Harbour so unique. As much a working waterway as a picture-perfect tourist attraction, the harbour plays a vital role in Sydney's daily routine and is the beautiful backdrop for special occasions like the New Year's Eve celebrations.

The cheapest way of enjoying the harbour is to take a ferry from Circular Quay – popular routes include Manly, Taronga Zoo and Watsons Bay – and there are many wonderful harbour walks (see page 135) skirting the foreshore.

You can also visit all five harbour islands (see Directions) but it's just as much fun to grab a bottle of wine, pick your own harbourside spot, and toast your good fortune.

Directions Captain Cook Cruises (9206 1111) operates daily harbour cruises from Wharf 6 at Circular Quay. The coffee cruise (2hrs 20mins) is the best, $33 adult; www.captcookcrus.com.au Sydney Ferries (131 500) operates daytime and evening cruises, $13 to $19 adult, and regular services from Circular Quay; www.sydneyferries.nsw.gov.au To visit any of the harbour islands, you must contact the National Parks and Wildlife Service (9247 5033); it offers tours or you can arrange your own transport (see water taxis, page 142).

Sydney Harbour from Cremorne Point.

The Bounty.

Life's a beach.

Campbells Cove.

The Rocks

Given the turbulent history of The Rocks, Sydney's first colonial settlement and the birthplace of modern Australia, it's a wonder the place is still standing.

From its humble origins as a makeshift camp for the convicts, sailors and soldiers of the First Fleet, The Rocks has survived the horrors of the early penal colony, bubonic plague, and the bulldozers of modern development to emerge as a cornerstone of Sydney's colonial heritage.

Bounded by the western shore of Circular Quay, the Harbour Bridge and Campbells Cove, The Rocks is a window on Sydney's past. Stroll through this maze of alleyways and cobblestone lanes and you'll see 200 years of history unfolding before your eyes.

The story of The Rocks begins with the raising of the Union Flag on January 26, 1788, establishing Sydney Cove as the farthest outpost of the British Empire, followed by rapid development.

Convict-built dockyards, wharfs and warehouses – Cadmans Cottage (built in 1816) is all that remains today – sprang up alongside timber-framed houses which followed the natural rock ledges of the cove. They were described as being "on the rocks" and the area has been known as The Rocks ever since.

The 19th century brought more commercial and residential growth, much of which can still be seen today, but led to severe overcrowding, prostitution and gangs. In the still of night in The Rocks, you can almost hear the ghosts of those turbulent times.

An outbreak of bubonic plague in 1900, spread by an infestation of ship rats, saw large areas of The Rocks demolished, and construction of the Harbour Bridge from 1924-32 cut another slice off it, but it was controversial development plans in the 1970s which nearly finished it off. But for the heroic resistance of residents and the Builders' Labourers Federation, The Rocks would not have survived, let alone become one of Sydney's premier commercial and tourist centres.

Framed by the city skyscrapers, The Rocks is a mix of old and new with more than 30 historic sites and some of the best hotels, restaurants, cafes, pubs, shops, galleries, museums, Aboriginal arts and crafts, and street entertainment in Sydney. It's a lively and bustling centre of activity day and night.

The best way to explore the area is on a guided or self-guided walking tour. George Street is the main commercial strip with the majority of historic sites between George and Cumberland streets.

Historic sandstone cottages and restored warehouses offer a range of excellent shopping while George Street plays host to the lively Rocks Market each weekend (10am-5pm).

Directions The Rocks lies on the western side of Circular Quay, easy walking distance from the city centre. The best approach is on foot via George Street. The Sydney Visitor Centre is at 106 George Street (9255 1788), open daily, 9am-6pm. The Rocks Walking Tours (9247 6678) depart from the visitor centre weekdays (10.30am, 12.30pm and 2.30pm), weekends (11.30am and 2pm), $12 adult. A self-guided walk map is also available.

magicmoment

Strolling along the boardwalk at Campbells Cove with its panorama of historic storehouses, the Harbour Bridge, Opera House, and replica of the Bounty.

mustsee

Susannah Place, an 1844 terrace at 58-64 Gloucester Street (9241 1893), now a delightful museum. Open weekends, 10am-5pm, $6 adult.

mustdo

Explore the maze of alleyways and old haunts of soldiers, sailors, convicts and merchants on a guided or self-guided walking tour.

Circular Quay

5

magicmoment

Sitting on the back of a ferry or harbour cruiser as it pulls in or out of Circular Quay. Day or night, the view is sensational.

mustsee

The new Customs House, with its excellent Aboriginal gallery and design studio Djamu, contemporary design gallery and store, and top-floor Cafe Sydney with its sweeping Quay views.

mustdo

The Writers' Walk, along East Circular Quay, with pavement plaques paying tribute to writers who have contributed to Australian literature.

You might think Circular Quay is little more than the ferry hub for Sydney Harbour but its history runs as deep as the water lapping against its sides. The landing place of the First Fleet on January 26, 1788, the Quay has played a vital role in the development of Sydney ever since.

While the first settlement grew around the Tank Stream, a creek which provided early Sydney's water supply and ran into the harbour, the Quay soon became a major transport hub lined with ships, boats, tugs and ferries.

It's not so different today. Day and night, Circular Quay bustles with marine activity whether it's one of the world's superliners docking at the Overseas Passenger Terminal on the western shore of the Quay or the public ferries and harbour cruisers which berth at the five main wharfs.

People usually go to Circular Quay to go somewhere else – it's also a major bus, rail and taxi hub – but there's plenty to see here as well. To the west of the Quay is First Fleet Park, home to the Museum of Contemporary Art, a dour Art Deco building which once housed the Maritime Services Board.

The museum has an interesting collection of modern art, changing exhibitions and a pleasant cafe with views to the Opera House. The park is always full of activity with street theatre, souvenir stalls and tourist crowds.

The main Circular Quay is an uninspiring collection of wharfs, restaurants, cafes and tourist shops but Customs Square in front of the Quay has great historical significance.

The colour-graded pavement in front of Customs House shows where the original waterline of Sydney Cove was – much of Circular Quay is on reclaimed land. Take time to visit Customs House, between Loftus and Young streets, now a major cultural and exhibition centre after a $24 million refurbishment of the 1845 building.

The apartments along East Circular Quay have been the subject of much controversy. The one nearest to the Opera House was dubbed The Toaster, given its resemblance to the electrical appliance, but the controversial development went ahead in the late 1990s despite enormous public opposition.

One good result is the row of restaurants, cafes and bars which now line the covered walkway to the Opera House (treat yourself to oysters and champagne at the Oyster Bar), a vast improvement on the office blocks of the past.

Day and night, the walkway buzzes with people heading to and from the Opera House in everything from dinner jackets to boardshorts. A good spot for people-watching.

Directions Circular Quay is the main hub for harbour ferries and a centre for buses and trains (131 500) as well as taxis. It's easy walking distance from Circular Quay to the Opera House, The Rocks and city centre. The Museum of Contemporary Art (9252 4033), on the west side of Circular Quay, is open daily except Tuesday, 10am-4pm, $9 adult; Customs House at Customs Square (9247 2285) is open daily, entry free.

Circular Quay, home to superliners and ferries.

The Lower Gardens in full bloom.

Royal Botanic Gardens

This is one of the treasures of Sydney – a wonderful collection of colourful gardens, the site of Sydney's first farm, and Australia's oldest scientific institution – situated right in the heart of the city. Bordered by the Opera House and city skyscrapers, Farm Cove and Woolloomooloo Bay, the gardens boast views that are as spectacular as the horticultural displays.

The land was cultivated shortly after the arrival of the First Fleet, hence the name Farm Cove, but proved to be unsatisfactory for agriculture. In 1792, Governor Arthur Phillip set the land aside as a reserve "for the Crown and the use of the Town of Sydney" but it wasn't until 1809 and the arrival of Governor Lachlan Macquarie that the gardens took on a more formal design.

Macquarie had part of the area, including the site of the first farm, enclosed with a stone wall and palings, then set about implementing his wife's plan for a road skirting Farm Cove and looping around what's now known as Mrs Macquarie's Point (folklore has it she enjoyed sitting on the point with its panoramic views of the harbour) and by 1816, the first botanic gardens were established.

The seawall at Farm Cove was added in the late 1800s – a great engineering feat of its time when the gardens were enlarged by five hectares of land reclaimed from the harbour – and by 1924 the site had assumed much of its present layout.

The collection of plants and trees is extraordinary, more than 7,000 species at last count from massive Moreton Bay fig trees to the eerie Palm Grove, famous for its colony of fruit bats which hang in the trees like Christmas decorations.

There are several individual gardens to explore. The Palace Garden was once home to the Garden Palace which housed the Great International Exhibition of 1879-80 but was destroyed by fire two years later.

The Rose Garden, Herb Garden, Rare and Threatened Plants Garden, Oriental Garden, Palm House, Fernery, First Farm, and Tropical Centre, with its striking glasshouse Pyramid and Arc, are all worth a visit or you can simply stroll through the park-like Lower Gardens with their superb views of the city and harbour.

Fauna and birdlife include brush-tailed possums, ibises, cockatoos, rainbow lorikeets and dusky moorhens.

The gardens are also home to the National Herbarium, the main botanical research centre in NSW containing about a million specimens, and the delightful Gardens Restaurant and Kiosk.

Directions The Royal Botanic Gardens lie to the east of the Opera House. There are nine gates, one by the Opera House, four on Macquarie Street and another four on Mrs Macquarie's Road. The park is free, open daily, 7am-sunset. The Visitor Centre (9231 8125) is open daily, 9.30am-4.30pm (except Christmas Day and Good Friday). There's a trackless train with commentary ($5 adult, board at the Opera House gate) if you don't want to walk the gardens.

6

magicmoment

Enjoying a picnic at Mrs Macquarie's Point with the panorama of the city, harbour, Opera House and Harbour Bridge laid out before you.

mustsee

The ancient Wollemi pine, thought to be extinct until found in the Blue Mountains in 1994. A specimen is close to the visitor centre.

mustdo

The free guided walk, daily at 10.30am (except public holidays), from the visitor centre. Audio headsets ($7) are also available for self-guided walks.

Macquarie Street

Like The Rocks, Macquarie Street is a window on Sydney's colonial history. One of the grandest streets in the city, it proudly bears the name of Governor Lachlan Macquarie, who did so much in the early 19th century to lay the foundations of the emerging colony.

Until Macquarie took over as governor in 1810, the town was a maze of narrow streets run largely by officials and soldiers cashing in on the rum monopoly.

The Scottish-born Macquarie, a man of vision and reform, quickly realised no civilised society could prosper without an orderly urban plan but he was continually frustrated by his colonial masters in London who didn't see any need for an architect in a penal colony.

Then along came Francis Greenway, a convict who had trained as an architect in England but had been sentenced to 14 years in New South Wales for forgery. Macquarie couldn't believe his luck, organised a "ticket of leave" allowing Greenway to work outside the convict system, and let him loose on his plans for Sydney.

The result can be seen today in many of the city's finest buildings, the best of which line Macquarie Street. Two of Greenway's architectural masterpieces are St James Church, built in 1820, and Hyde Park Barracks (1817), which face each other at the southern end of the street near Hyde Park. Georgian in style and classically simple, the barracks – originally convict quarters and now a history museum – and church complement each other perfectly.

Alongside the barracks lie The Mint and State Parliament House, two beautiful colonnaded edifices built in 1816 as wings of Greenway's original Sydney Hospital.

The Mint, most recently a museum of decorative arts, is closed but you can wander through State Parliament House (open Monday to Friday, 9am-4.30pm). It claims to be the world's oldest continually operating parliament building, a seat of government since 1827.

Wedged in between is the still operating Sydney Hospital, dating from the 1880s. Stop to rub the snout of Il Porcellino, the Little Boar, a gift from Italy which reputedly brings good luck.

Alongside State Parliament House is the State Library and imposing Mitchell Library, housing one of the best collections of early records on Australia, including the journals of Captain Cook, Sir Joseph Banks and the ship's log of Captain Bligh, of the Bounty fame.

At the northern end of Macquarie Street lies the Sydney Conservatorium of Music, originally built in 1819 (by Greenway again) as the stables of Government House. The brooding castellated mansion in the Royal Botanic Gardens has been home to successive State governors but is now mainly used for public functions.

The west side of the street is less inspiring, lined with apartments, offices, medical surgeries (this is the Harley Street of Sydney), churches and government buildings, but it's a neat counterpoint to Greenway's grand vision.

Directions Macquarie Street runs from the Opera House alongside the Royal Botanic Gardens to Hyde Park.

Hotel Inter.Continental.

The art gallery is an artwork in itself.

Art Gallery of NSW

For anyone with even a passing interest in art, the Art Gallery of NSW should be high on a must-see list of Sydney attractions. The gallery, housed in a grand Romanesque sandstone building overlooking the lawns of The Domain, is guardian to a wonderful collection of art.

Forget any notions of a stuffy museum with old paintings gathering dust. Step through the imposing columns of the entrance and you'll enter a modern, vibrant and constantly changing gallery containing some of the most important art in Australia.

Spread over five levels, the gallery's principal strength lies in the collections of Australian, Asian, European (particularly 19th century), and contemporary art.

The Yiribana Aboriginal and Torres Strait Islander Gallery is another key feature with one of the most important permanent displays of Aboriginal art, complemented by daily performances and regular exhibitions by leading Aboriginal artists.

As well as paintings and sculptures, the gallery also has an extensive collection of photography, prints, drawings and watercolours, and an ongoing program of more than 30 exhibitions each year from Australia and around the world.

More than a million people pass through the collections each year.

The beautiful Old Courts, the original exhibition halls on the Ground Level, are home to an extensive collection of 19th and 20th century Australian art, including iconic masterpieces by Tom Roberts, Arthur Streeton, Frederick McCubbin, Grace Cossington Smith, William Dobell, Sidney Nolan, Russell Drysdale and Arthur Boyd.

The Old Courts also contain European paintings from the 15th to the early 20th century, including Rubens, Tiepolo and Canaletto, and a rich collection of Victorian, Edwardian and French Impressionist paintings.

The Asian collection is on Level One, contemporary art, prints, drawings and photography displays are on Level Two, and the Yiribana (meaning "This Way") collection is on Level Three.

The gallery also has a sculpture terrace, a very good shop, theatre, cafe and brasserie. The information desk and daily tour board are by the Gallery Shop.

The Art Gallery of NSW fronts onto The Domain, ideal for a relaxing walk after you've had your fill of Roberts and Rubens. The Pavilion on the Park, across the road from the gallery, has a pleasant cafe and restaurant overlooking The Domain.

Prepare to set aside a morning or afternoon for this wonderful art gallery because once you're inside, you'll be hooked.

Directions The Art Gallery of NSW is on Art Gallery Road, The Domain. Bus 441 runs between the gallery and Queen Victoria Building (131 500). It's a pleasant five-minute walk from St James and Martin Place train stations and a 15-minute walk from the city centre.

The gallery (9225 1744) is open daily, 10am-5pm (except Good Friday and Christmas Day), entry free. There are daily tours, audio guides and exhibition tours; www.artgallery.nsw.gov.au

magicmoment

Viewing the wonderful collection of 19th and 20th century Australian art, featuring works by Tom Roberts, Arthur Streeton, Sidney Nolan and William Dobell.

mustsee

The collection of Aboriginal paintings and sculptures in the Yiribana Gallery, especially the 17 Pukamani Poles, commissioned in 1958.

mustdo

One of the free daily hour-long tours (9225 1744), revealing the highlights of the collections and art gallery.

Hyde Park

9

magicmoment

Strolling under the cathedral-like arch of fig trees, extending almost the full length of Hyde Park.

mustsee

The poignant Anzac War Memorial and Pool of Reflection at the southern end of the park.

mustdo

An evening walk around the edge of Hyde Park to see the avenue of fairy lights. You might even see possums scampering between the trees.

Like an oasis in the heart of the city, Hyde Park offers a calm and peaceful haven from Sydney's ever-growing traffic and crowds. Encompassing about seven hectares, or four city blocks, it's a fraction of the size and royal grandeur of its London counterpart but it's a popular drawcard for office workers, shoppers and tourists.

Each morning, the park is a hive of activity with joggers pounding the lawns, shop assistants scurrying to the neighbouring David Jones and other city department stores, and elderly men and women congregating at the giant chequerboard by the entrance to St James train station for a game of chess.

The park really comes into its own at lunchtime when crowds descend on the neatly clipped lawns to enjoy a sandwich, a gossip and a few rays of sun. There's a distinctly European atmosphere as people flock to the graceful Archibald Fountain, dipping their feet in the cool water when the summer temperatures soar.

The fountain, designed by French sculptor Francois Sicard in 1932, commemorates Australian and French Allied troops who fought together in World War I. The figures of Apollo, Pan, Theseus and Diana lend the fountain a thoroughly romantic air.

The fountain is in sharp contrast to the stark and imposing Anzac War Memorial (1934) at the southern end of Hyde Park. The poignant Art Deco monument in pink and grey granite has a beautifully carved bronze memorial to the Unknown Soldier as its centrepiece, an eternal flame, and friezes commemorating all Australians who have served their country at war. The memorial stands beside a poplar-lined Pool of Reflection.

The monument houses a small but interesting exhibition on Australia's military history and the Last Post is sounded each day at 11am. There's added poignancy with the pine trees near the monument. They were grown from seeds taken from Gallipoli in Turkey, one of the bloodiest battlegrounds for Australian troops in World War I.

On the west side of the park lies Elizabeth Street, a wide boulevard of designer stores, office blocks and hotels. On the east side lies the imposing St Mary's Cathedral, one of the largest in the world, completed in 1882 but only recently crowned with its spires.

A little further south along College Street is the Australian Museum (see page 133) which has permanent and changing exhibitions on a range of natural history topics and is especially good if you're travelling with children.

A word of warning about Hyde Park. The central avenue of trees sparkle at night with very pretty fairy lights but it's also a magnet for drug addicts and drunks. You can view Hyde Park at night from the roadside but wander through it in daylight hours only.

Directions Hyde Park lies in the centre of the city between Elizabeth and College streets. It's an easy walk from anywhere in the central business district. The underground St James and Museum train stations lead directly into Hyde Park.

Archibald Fountain.

There's no other store quite like it.

David Jones

There are newer, and arguably better, shops in Sydney but the advertising slogan *There's No Other Store Like David Jones* sums up its position in the retail heart of the city.

Billing itself as the world's oldest department store still trading under the same name, the 162-year-old David Jones is to Sydney what Harrods is to London and Bloomingdale's is to New York.

The grande dame of department stores, holding court over Elizabeth and Market streets, is a Sydney institution with a proud retailing history dating back to 1838. Tradition is writ large across this fashion and food emporium, one of Australia's great stores and a popular tourist attraction in its own right.

From the marble floors to the vast sprays of flowers, David Jones oozes old-fashioned style and service. A pianist tickles the ivories on the ground floor of the Elizabeth Street store while cosmetic experts tend to willing faces.

On other levels, black-clad shop assistants scurry between mannequins and counters while the Food Hall, in the basement of the Market Street store, bustles with customers.

The department store started life in George Street with David Jones, a Welsh-born retailer trained in London opening "a large and commodious premises" selling "buckskins, ginghams, waist-coatings, silks, cottons, diaper rugs" and other merchandise imported from London. The store quickly grew, introducing the European concept of a department store, establishing a mail order service, and becoming the shopping choice of the landed gentry.

The twin Elizabeth and Market Street stores opened in 1927 and 1938 respectively and massive growth in the second half of the century saw the chain expand to more than 30 department stores nationwide. The city store remains the flagship of the company.

In true emporium style, fashion is only a part of the David Jones portfolio. The store also has one of the best food halls in Sydney with top-quality local and imported produce. You can shop for cheeses, meats, fish, poultry, fruit and vegetables, domestic and imported gourmet goods, and tuck into a dozen oysters and a glass of chardonnay at the popular oyster bar.

There are regular fashion shows in the Elizabeth Street store, morning tea, lunch and Sunday brunch can be taken in the elegant Park Terrace Restaurant, and the cosmetics department on the ground floor of the Elizabeth Street store is a haze of fresh flowers and perfume.

The menswear department is in the Market Street store above the Food Hall.

There's stiff competition from the refurbished Grace Bros, at the George Street end of Market Street, and other local and international retail outlets but as the saying goes, there really is no other store quite like David Jones.

Directions David Jones city store is on the corner of Elizabeth and Market streets, across from Hyde Park. The men's store is on the corner of Castlereagh and Market streets. The store (9266 5544) is open daily, 9.30am-6pm, Thursday until 9pm, Saturday 9am-6pm, Sunday 11am-5pm.

magicmoment

Searching for that special something in the haze of flowers, perfume and soft music on the ground floor of the main Elizabeth Street store.

mustsee

The annual David Jones Spring Flower Show in September when the store is in full bloom.

mustdo

Morning tea, lunch or Sunday brunch in the elegant Park Terrace Restaurant on Level 7 (9266 5641).

AMP Tower Centrepoint

⓫

magicmoment

Taking in the panoramic views of Sydney from the Observation Level, towering 250 metres above the city.

mustsee

The steel-sculpture athletes on top of the tower, AMP's tribute to the Sydney 2000 Olympic and Paralympic Games.

mustdo

Use the VIP discount card, free with your tower entry pass, for some retail therapy in the Centrepoint shopping complex.

How's your head for heights? One of the finest views in (and of) Sydney is from the AMP Tower, in the heart of the city, but you'll have to rise 250 metres to a cloud-touching observation deck to see it.

Standing like a beacon to modern achievement, the AMP Tower (popularly known as Centrepoint) is Sydney's equivalent of the CN Tower in Toronto and Empire State Building in New York except it's nowhere near as tall. It's not even in the top 10 of the world's tallest buildings.

It is, however, the tallest building in Australia, boasts the highest observation deck in the southern hemisphere and, at 305 metres from spire to pavement, offers breathtaking views on a clear day from the Pacific Ocean in the east to the Blue Mountains in the west.

No visit to Sydney would be complete without a trip up the tower, a torch-like spindle holding telecommunications equipment, a four-level observation turret, two revolving restaurants, 10 floors of offices and more than 150 shops. The tower is held in place by 56 stabilising cables which, laid end to end, would stretch from Sydney to New Zealand.

While it might look a little fragile, the tower is capable of withstanding extreme wind conditions and earthquakes (tested by the minor tremors which rumble Sydney occasionally) and has been ranked as one of the safest buildings in the world. Conceived in 1968 and completed in 1981, the tower dominates the city skyline with its striking golden turret glistening in the sun atop a licorice-stick pole.

It's even more dramatic with the three steel sculptures – designed to represent a runner, a wheelchair basketball player and gymnast – placed on top of the turret (in a delicate operation by helicopter) as a tribute to the Sydney 2000 Olympic and Paralympic Games. The tower also has a message panel announcing a daily countdown to the event.

It's the views, though, which attract the one million annual visitors who are whisked up to the observation deck in 40 heart-stopping seconds by three super-fast lifts.

There are displays and directions, as well as coin-operated binoculars, to give you a better view of the city, but all you need do is wander around the observation deck windows (washed by machine rather than terrified window cleaners) to see Sydney in all its glory.

Climb the tower early in your visit and it will provide you with an excellent overview of the layout of the city. Two revolving restaurants (a la carte and self-service) offer standard tourist fare but, views aside, you'll eat better elsewhere.

Directions The AMP Tower Centrepoint is at 100 Market Street, next to the City Centre monorail station. Proceed to the Podium Level where you'll find lifts to the Observation Level, $10 adult, $4.50 child. The tower (9231 1000) is open daily, 9am-10.30pm, Saturday to 11.30pm. The shopping centre is open daily, 9am-6pm, Thursday to 8pm, Sunday 11am-4pm; www.centrepoint.com.au

A towering tribute to the Olympic Games.

The queen of Sydney shopping centres.

Queen Victoria Building

This stately building has been buffeted by the winds of change so many times in a chequered 100-year history, it's a wonder she still exists. But, like a dowager duchess standing firm, proud and regal against the tide of history, the Queen Victoria Building has survived against the odds to become one of Sydney's architectural treasures.

This is a true riches to rags and back to riches tale which would surely amuse the crusty old queen who lent her name to the building. It begins in 1892 with civic leaders proposing a Romanesque palace to house a new central city market. Five years, 4.5 million bricks, 3,000 tonnes of steel, mountains of sandstone and granite, a grand central dome, several minor domes, a general market, concert hall and public library later, the building was officially declared open.

But dark days were just around the corner and by 1916 the market tenants and city council were rowing over rent levels. Over the next 67 years, the building deteriorated badly as successive city councils modified it, turned it into the headquarters of the Electricity Department, and even recommended demolition on three separate occasions.

It was only due to a lack of finances and the intervention of the National Trust, which deemed the building was "essential to the nation's heritage", that it was spared the bulldozers. Restoration plans came to nought until 1980 when a Malaysian consortium stepped in with a submission to restore the Queen Victoria Building to retail splendour.

It took $75 million and three years of stripping, sifting, scraping, excavating and digging to remove the years of remodelling and in 1986 Sydney gained an elegant new shopping centre. It reigns majestically to this day with locals and tourists pouring through the 200 quality stores, restaurants and attractions each day.

The QVB has four beautiful galleries, trimmed with stained glass, timber balustrades and tiled floors, all set under a glass dome and original 19th century staircase, the location for a massive Christmas tree in the festive season.

The building also contains several public exhibits, including a wishing well, a time capsule presented by Queen Elizabeth II, an Imperial Jade Carriage, a memorial to the 96 Australians who have been awarded the Victoria Cross, the Great Australian Clock (see Must See), and the Royal Automata Clock, made by Thwaites and Reed, the keepers of London's Big Ben.

Pride of place, however, goes to a bronze statue of Queen Victoria, which once stood outside the Irish Parliament in Dublin and was a gift to Sydney from the people of Ireland. It sits in regal splendour at the Druitt Street entrance.

Directions The Queen Victoria Building lies in the heart of the city, bordered by George, Market, York and Druitt streets. Town Hall train station leads into the lower ground floor and buses stop in George and York streets. Shopping hours are 9am-6pm, Thursday to 9pm, Sunday 11am-5pm; www.qvb.com.au

⑫

magicmoment

Standing beneath the magnificent central glass dome and original 19th century staircase. It's especially pretty during the Christmas season.

mustsee

The Great Australian Clock, the world's largest animated clock, with more than 100 scenes of Australian history. It hangs at the northern end of the building.

mustdo

A guided tour (9264 9209), daily 11.30am and 2.30pm, from the ground floor customer service desk, $5 adult. Private tours can also be booked.

Darling Harbour

13

magicmoment

Stepping through the archway of the beautiful Chinese Garden of Friendship into another world.

mustsee

Sydney Aquarium, Australian National Maritime Museum and Powerhouse Museum (see pages 131 and 133).

mustdo

Lunch or dinner at one of the Harbourside or Cockle Bay Wharf restaurants. Harbour yacht tours also operate from Darling Harbour.

Rising like a phoenix from the ashes of a disused goods yard, Darling Harbour has emerged to become one of Sydney's premier tourist and entertainment centres. Sprawled around Cockle Bay, on the western side of the central business district, it's a vast complex of shops, hotels, restaurants, cafes, museums, gardens and themed attractions with the emphasis firmly on family entertainment.

The collection of 10 major attractions – Sydney Aquarium, National Maritime Museum, Powerhouse Museum, Panasonic IMAX Theatre, Darling Walk, Sega World, Harbourside Shopping Centre, Star City Casino, Chinese Garden of Friendship and Cockle Bay Wharf – reads like a Who's Who of the entertainment world.

Throw in seven hotels, separate convention, exhibition and entertainment centres (which will be venues for weightlifting, wrestling, judo, boxing, volleyball and fencing at the Sydney 2000 Olympic Games), a monorail skirting the entire complex, the sparkling waters of Cockle Bay, a panoramic city skyline, and you have a "theme park" to rival Disneyworld.

Opened in 1988 as part of the Bicentennial celebrations, Darling Harbour has not been without its problems. The Harbourside Shopping Centre, once filled with tacky tourist shops and fast-food outlets, almost became Sydney's white elephant as locals shunned the development in favour of more upmarket and accessible shopping centres.

It has been a long time in the making but Darling Harbour has finally come good. A $60 million refurbishment has turned Harbourside into a contemporary and vibrant shopping centre with beautiful stores like The Cotton Store and Gavala Aboriginal Art and Cultural Centre, and a range of quality Australian-made products from jewellery to ceramics, fashion, homewares and sports gear.

Harbourside, open seven days, is home to more than 100 stores and restaurants and offers free outdoor family entertainment at weekends.

The multi-million-dollar Cockle Bay Wharf, on the city side of Darling Harbour, has also given the complex a significant boost with its five-star and themed restaurants, cafes, bars and nightclub luring locals as well as tourists back into the complex.

Just behind Darling Harbour is Star City, Sydney's casino-hotel. It may not be to everyone's taste, with its fake palm trees, desert rocks and rainforests screaming Viva Las Vegas rather than Casino Royale, but it's a fine hotel (9657 8393), has good restaurants and entertainment venues, and lends a sparkle to Darling Harbour at night.

Our pick of attractions are the Sydney Aquarium, featuring underwater shark-viewing walkways and an excellent Great Barrier Reef exhibit, the Panasonic IMAX Theatre, National Maritime Museum and Powerhouse Museum, taking visitors through the centuries of human achievement. Hours of fun for the whole family.

Directions Darling Harbour is just to the west of the city centre. You can walk there from Market Street across Pyrmont Bridge, take the monorail, the light rail, or Matilda Cruises' Rocket ferry service from Circular Quay. www.darlingharbour.com.au

Harbourside.

Shark tunnel at Sydney Aquarium.

The monorail.

A culture within a culture in the heart of the city.

Chinatown

Wander among the weekend crowds of Sydney's Chinatown and it might for all the world be Hong Kong, Beijing or Shanghai.

Wizened old women hobble along the street clutching string bags bulging with food. Portly businessmen, with more than a passing resemblance to Buddha, yell into mobile phones. Young girls giggle at posters of Chinese film stars leering from video shop windows.

Rows of glistening barbecued ducks hang upside down in restaurant windows. Neon lights, a jumble of Chinese symbols and restaurant names like Marigold, House of Guangzhou and Jing May flicker into life as the sun goes down, while the aromas of stir-fry, chilli, ginger and dim sum waft onto the street.

It's hard to escape the Asian influence in Sydney. Immigrants from China, Singapore, Malaysia, Thailand, Japan and a host of other Asian nations have carved a deep and abiding mark – not least in the myriad restaurants across the city – on Sydney's cultural landscape.

The Chinese have had a long association with Sydney. Two Chinese cooks were said to have been on the First Fleet when it arrived in 1788 and their culinary skills were obviously handed down through the generations. The local Chinese population is now estimated at 200,000, lending the city an exotically Oriental air, most notably in Chinatown.

It's nowhere near the size of Chinatowns in other international cities but it is growing rapidly, spreading over a large area bordered by Liverpool, Quay and George Streets in the heart of the city. It is no less busy, vibrant and colourful as other Chinatowns and, during Chinese New Year in February, takes on a life all its own.

The traditional heart of Chinatown is in Dixon Street, an uninspiring enclave of good and bad restaurants with stately Chinese gates at either end. Earth from Guangdong Province has been buried around the gates as a symbolic gesture that Australia is a new home.

From Dixon Street, Chinatown snakes around Hay Street, alongside Paddy's Market and Market City in Haymarket, and past rows of Chinese restaurants to Thomas Street. On a busy night, you'd be forgiven for thinking you're in Hong Kong.

Eating is a Chinese obsession which means you'll never go hungry. Check to see which restaurants are fullest for the best indication of quality of food but it's largely a case of take your pick in Chinatown. Some of the mega-restaurants like Kam Fook (see Must Do) are a treat.

There's good shopping in Paddy's Market and Market City – and the Burlington Centre Supermarket in Thomas Street, with its range of Chinese goods, is a sight to behold – but half the fun of Chinatown is simply wandering the streets and soaking up the atmosphere.

Directions Chinatown lies west of George Street, bordered by Liverpool, Sussex, Dixon, Hay, Thomas and Quay streets, and is easy walking distance from the central business district and Darling Harbour. The monorail and light rail both stop at Haymarket.

magicmoment

Losing yourself in the bustling crowds of Chinatown and watching a culture within a culture at work and play.

mustsee

The Burlington Centre Supermarket, in Thomas Street, with 12,000 assorted items from bottles of sake to fresh abalone and Chinese herbs.

mustdo

Yum cha at Kam Fook, a bustling 800-seat Cantonese restaurant on Level 3, Market City, Hay Street, usually packed with Chinese families (9211 8988).

Sydney Fish Market

15

magicmoment
Browsing around the seafood counters, brimming with lobsters, prawns, oysters, giant tuna, parrot fish and other catches of the day.

mustsee
The prawn trawlers, fishing boats and pelicans at the market wharf, a pleasant spot for a seafood picnic.

mustdo
A two-hour cooking class, four-hour workshop, or early morning breakfast tour (7am-9am including a tour of the auction room) at the Sydney Seafood School (9552 2180).

Given its proximity to ocean, rivers and lakes, it's no surprise that Sydney is famous for its seafood. From plump Sydney rock oysters to fillets of barramundi, there's barely a hotel or restaurant in the city which doesn't have some kind of seafood on its menu.

Little wonder then that the Sydney Fish Market, located at Blackwattle Bay on the west side of Darling Harbour, is a constant hive of activity, offering a variety of seafood second only to Tokyo's Tsukiji Market, as well as the largest seafood auction house in the southern hemisphere and an authentic fishermen's wharf.

Throw in six of the city's largest seafood retailers, a sushi bar, one of the famous Doyle's seafood restaurants, a colony of pelicans, a cast of characters from the local fishing industry, and you've got one of Sydney's great attractions.

Every day, tens of thousands of crates of fish, much of it caught that morning, pours into the Sydney Fish Market to be cleaned, weighed, auctioned, packed in ice, and dispatched to the dining tables of hotels, restaurants and homes throughout the city.

Lobsters, oysters, scallops and mussels, crayfish and Balmain bugs, giant tuna, red emperor and Atlantic salmon are among more than 100 varieties packed nose to tail-fin on counters laden with shoals of seafood.

From 5.30am, the market is buzzing with about 170 registered buyers filling the seafood auction room – there's a public viewing area to watch the auction – and trading 2,800 crates (around 70,000kg) of fish. By 7am, the first of the market shops are open and selling to eager customers.

Privatised in 1994, the Sydney Fish Market is a joint venture company, half of which is owned by the tenants on the site, the other half owned by the catching sector of the NSW fishing industry.

More than 16 million kilograms of seafood are sold at the market every year.

It's wonderful for browsing and dining and the ideal place to pick up prawns, oysters, sushi (rice and fish or cucumber rolled in seaweed) and sashimi (slivers of raw tuna and salmon) for a picnic, or a whole fish for a barbecue.

The market is also home to the Sydney Seafood School where you can learn about cooking fish and the workings of the market (see Must Do). In a city hooked on seafood, this is the place to enjoy a classic Sydney experience.

Directions The Sydney Fish Market is at Blackwattle Bay, on the west side of Darling Harbour. The light rail runs from Central or Haymarket to the Fish Market stop. Bus 443 runs from Circular Quay and 501 runs from Town Hall and Central. There's a summer ferry service from December to Easter (weekends and public holidays only) from Circular Quay (131 500). The market has its own car park, $3 for the first two hours. The shops are open daily, 7am-4pm (except Christmas Day). Fish Line (9552 2180); www.sydneyfishmarket.com.au

Catches of the day at the Sydney Fish Market.

Sydney Observatory

Observatory Hill

Australia has one of the best night skies in the world but, under the bright lights of Sydney, it's often hard to see the constellations. Visit the Sydney Observatory on a cloudless night and you're guaranteed to have stars in your eyes.

The oldest observatory in Australia, it's also a fascinating museum for anyone with even the faintest interest in astronomy. Keen stargazers have been visiting this charming Victorian observatory for more than 140 years eager to look deep into the big black yonder.

While it's no longer at the cutting edge of modern astronomy, it's a wonderful centre for learning about and exploring the stars of the Great Southern Sky.

There are two main telescopes. The historic lens telescope in the south dome dates from 1874 and is the oldest regularly used telescope in Australia. The mirror telescope in the north dome is computer-controlled and incorporates the latest in precision technology.

Combined with tours, lectures, exhibitions, a small planetarium, and night viewing of the stars (weather permitting), it makes for a pleasant evening excursion. As it stands on the highest point of Sydney at Millers Point, next to The Rocks, it also boasts good views of the twinkling lights of the city.

The Observatory's main exhibition, By the Light of the Southern Stars, ranges from observations of the Transit of Venus by Captain Cook to the ongoing work of other Australian observatories and an explanation of the basics of astronomy.

The Observatory, part of the Powerhouse Museum, also features an exhibition of stars from the Aboriginal perspective and tells how Australia's first astronomers used the sky and stars in their Dreamtime stories.

A short walk from the Observatory is the National Trust Centre, housing the SH Ervin Gallery, a cafe and gift shop, while the five-star Observatory Hotel, part of the Orient-Express chain of hotels, lies on the west side of the hill in Kent Street.

If you visit during the day, take time to wander the historic streets around Millers Point, named after the flour mill which once stood on Observatory Hill.

Walk up Argyle Street, through the imposing Argyle Cut – a convict-built tunnel connecting The Rocks with Millers Point – and you'll find the lovely Garrison Church (1848), rows of historic houses, tree-lined squares, and two of the oldest pubs in Sydney.

The Lord Nelson, on the corner of Argyle and Kent streets, and Hero of Waterloo, on the corner of Windmill and Lower Fort streets, both claim to be Sydney's "oldest continually operating pub". Leave the hair-splitting to the historians and settle in for an ice-cold beer.

Directions You can walk to Observatory Hill from The Rocks, via Argyle Street, then sharp left into Watson Road. Buses 431 and 432 run from Circular Quay and buses 343 and 431 from Wynyard train station (131 500). The Sydney Observatory is open daily, 10am-5pm (except Christmas Day). Free entry by day, $8 adult at night. Bookings essential (9217 0485); www.phm.gov.au

16

magicmoment

Gazing out at the stars and planets of the Great Southern Sky at a night viewing.

mustsee

The historic streets of Millers Point, surrounding Observatory Hill, especially the beautiful 1848 convict-built Garrison Church.

mustdo

A two-hour evening tour of the Observatory, including a talk, exhibition and viewing through the telescopes (9217 0485).

Fort Denison

magicmoment

Clambering onto the ramparts of Fort Denison and taking in the 360-degree panorama of Sydney Harbour. Spare a thought for the wretched prisoners who were once incarcerated on this tiny island.

mustsee

Fort Denison from a ferry or harbour cruiser.

mustdo

A guided tour with the National Parks and Wildlife Service (see Directions). Note: Fort Denison is closed in 1999 and early 2000 for renovations.

It seems incongruous that a Boys' Own fort sits impassively in the middle of peaceful Sydney Harbour but the city had to protect itself from foreign invaders somehow – or at least had to be seen to be protecting itself.

Fort Denison, also known as Pinchgut, began life as a solitary rock where wretched convicts who fell foul of the law in the earliest days of colonial rule were sent as punishment.

The first "inmate", Thomas Hill, was left there exposed to the elements for a week in 1788 for stealing a handful of biscuits.

A steady stream of prisoners was dumped on the island over the next few years, with barely anyone keeping watch over them except the hungry sharks which inhabited the harbour. Not surprisingly, they proved a powerful deterrent for any hapless prisoner aiming to swim to freedom.

The origins of the name Pinchgut are unclear. Some say it derives from a nautical term for the narrowing of a body of water at a certain place, as with this part of Sydney Harbour. Others say the bread-and-water rations for the prisoners were so meagre that their "guts" were literally "pinched". The latter explanation seems much more apt.

From the mid-1800s, the island was progressively fortified with the imposing Martello tower and rows of cannons added to the ramparts – largely due to fears of Russian expansion in the Pacific region – although a salvo from Fort Denison would probably be like hitting an invader over the head with a feather duster.

Today, Fort Denison lies at peace, a much-loved remnant of Sydney's colonial history enjoying pride of place in the harbour, just to the east of the Opera House.

Two centuries of water erosion and general pollution have badly affected the fort's foundations and a major restoration program was put in place in mid-1999 to repair the damage and expand the tourist facilities on the island.

The National Parks and Wildlife Service will offer guided tours and access to Fort Denison once it reopens to the public (see Directions).

The highlight of a visit to Fort Denison is visual rather than historical. The 360-degree view of the harbour and city is one of the best panoramas in Sydney, so a guided tour is a must once it reopens. Otherwise you can view the ramparts from a ferry or harbour cruiser.

For the most part, Fort Denison stands undisturbed, except for flocks of seagulls which seem to treat it like a rookery. Private parties are occasionally held on the fort, lending the brooding pile a festive air, but its heyday as prison and protector have long since past.

Directions Fort Denison is closed for renovations but is scheduled to reopen in April 2000. Once it does, the best way to see it is on a guided tour with the National Parks and Wildlife Service; tours depart from Cadmans Cottage on the west side of Circular Quay.
For details, contact (9247 5033).

The imposing Martello Tower and magnificent view from the fort.

Fabulous frocks at the Gay and Lesbian Mardi Gras.

Oxford Street

Time to slip on the spandex because this is the playground for gay Sydney. Oxford Street has some terrific restaurants, cafes, bars and nightclubs but the lifestyle here is unashamedly alternative.

While Kings Cross wears its heart on its sleaze, Oxford Street worships at the temple of hedonism, a frothy cocktail of frou-frou, feather boas and fabulous frocks, big hair, false eyelashes, glossy lipstick, spangly micro-dresses and towering stilettos – and that's just the men.

During the annual Gay and Lesbian Mardi Gras Festival in February, add a Central Casting collection of shaved heads, black leather, glittery hot pants, an "order" of nuns-in-drag known as The Sisters of Perpetual Indulgence, more muscle boys than you could poke a G-string at, and it's *The Adventures of Priscilla, Queen of the Desert* in living technicolour.

Given Australia's macho image, it might come as a surprise that a gay community not only survives but thrives along this pink brick road but Sydney has one of the biggest gay communities in the world (second only to San Francisco), a vocal and colourful feature on the city's political, cultural and sexual landscape.

While "queer-bashing" is still a bloodsport among Sydney's homophobe gangs, Oxford Street is generally safer, more relaxed and more fun than Kings Cross. Some bars and clubs are for gays only; others are open to everyone. All are loud and lively with the thud of techno music beating across the street throughout the night.

Oxford Street is not an exclusively gay haunt. By day, it's a busy commercial centre with groovy fashion and homeware stores, and by night the restaurants around Taylor Square, Crown Street and along Oxford Street are usually packed with people of all persuasions.

Facing Taylor Square is Darlinghurst Courthouse, built in 1842, behind which is the old Darlinghurst Jail, now an art college. The Jewish Museum on the corner of Darlinghurst Road and Burton Street is well worth a visit (see page 133).

The highlight of Sydney's gay calendar is the annual Gay and Lesbian Mardi Gras Festival which runs through February and culminates in the Mardi Gras Parade, billed as the world's biggest gay parade and one of the city's largest and most colourful events.

The parade attracts a crowd of around 500,000 and generates millions of dollars in tourism for the city.

Free papers such as *Capital Q* and *Sydney Star Observer* have extensive listings of all the city's gay venues and events but be warned: straying into the dimly lit streets surrounding Oxford Street may be an invitation to danger. Stick to the bright lights and enjoy the passing parade.

Directions Oxford Street runs from the south-east corner of Hyde Park through Darlinghurst and Paddington to Centennial Park. The Darlinghurst strip of shops, restaurants, bars, nightclubs and cafes is easy walking distance from the city centre. Buses 380 and 382 run from Circular Quay, 378 from Central train station along Oxford Street (131 500).

18

magicmoment

Sitting at an outdoor table at any of Oxford Street's cafes and bars and watching gay Sydney at play. Wig, mini-dress and stilettos optional.

mustsee

The annual Gay and Lesbian Mardi Gras Parade, usually the first Saturday in March.

mustdo

A shopping raid on the groovy fashion and homeware stores along Oxford Street, Darlinghurst and Paddington.

Kings Cross

19

magicmoment

Er...

mustsee

Visit the Korean Bath House in the Hotel Capital, 111 Darlinghurst Road (9358 2755), for a traditional sauna and body scrub. Be prepared to be steamed, scrubbed and soaked to within an inch of your life.

mustdo

Late-night drinks at the Bourbon and Beefsteak, 24 Darlinghurst Road (9358 1144), the legendary Kings Cross nightclub where all life (high and low) is on show.

Everything you've heard about Kings Cross, even the stuff you can't quite believe, is true. This racy enclave of sex shops, massage parlours, strip clubs, video lounges, neon lights, prostitutes, spruikers and drug addicts is the sleaze capital of Australia and is not for the faint-hearted.

On any given night, when the sun dips below the horizon, the Cross is bathed in a sea of red light which washes up William Street, swirls around the giant neon Coke sign at the intersection of Victoria Street, and floods along Darlinghurst Road.

Its wake is filled with hundreds, often thousands, of eager thrill-seekers, party animals, bikies, street-sellers, gawping tourists, and the flotsam and jetsam of the city's low-life who flock to the Cross like moths to a candle. The place all but comes with a Government Health Warning, no surprise given it has a criminal record that would make Al Capone blush.

No newspaper headline screaming about an underworld shooting, politician-caught-in-brothel sex scandal, drug bust, illegal gambling, prostitution racket or police corruption is complete without the name Kings Cross tagged on the end.

There is a softer side to the Cross which is home to some great cafes and restaurants, leafy squares (the El Alamein Fountain in Fitzroy Gardens is a centrepiece) and fine Victorian architecture. By day, it appears much like any other suburb, its pavements filled with local residents, office workers and tourists.

Kings Cross also has many good hotels and backpacker hostels but the bohemian atmosphere is confined largely to daylight hours. Its descent into vice began in the Vietnam era when the area was a favourite haunt for US and Australian servicemen in search of R&R, and the place is still a magnet for the crews of visiting navy ships.

We don't want to put you off the place – a wander along Darlinghurst Road after dark can provide you with hours of lascivious entertainment – but if you venture into this seedy strip, keep your wits about you at all times.

There's an inherently sinister edge to Kings Cross, with its nightly cast of drunks, addicts, pickpockets and prostitutes. You can buy anything from a cuddly toy koala to a tattoo but if you don't want to take home an unwelcome souvenir of Sydney, steer clear of the sex haunts.

If Kings Cross isn't your scene, the leafy and genteel Potts Point and Elizabeth Bay are next door. Wolloomooloo is home to the Garden Island naval base and the legendary Harry's Cafe de Wheels in Cowper Wharf Road, a mobile pie van loved by locals and visiting celebrities. Harry's late-night pies are a Sydney institution.

Directions Kings Cross is at the top end of William Street and encompasses Victoria Street, Darlinghurst Road, Bayswater Road and surrounding streets. The underground Kings Cross train station is in Victoria Street; bus 311 runs from Circular Quay and Central train station to the Cross (131 500).

AWAY

leevemasters TATTOO

STRIPPERAM nite spot

Kings Cross, by day and night.

North Shore and Northern Beaches

City centre

Y ou don't have to venture too far onto Sydney's north shore to believe the gods were smiling when they created this chunk of real estate. This is where Sydney's serious money lives, a sprawling *House and Gardens* confection of beautiful homes, tree-lined avenues, shiny cars, smart shops, chic restaurants, and the occasional marina to park the boat which simply won't fit in the three-car garage.

From Kirribilli, nestled beside the Harbour Bridge on the tip of the lower north shore, to Ku-ring-gai Chase National Park in the far north of the city, northside residents enjoy a thoroughly relaxed and comfortable lifestyle in one of the world's most beautiful urban settings.

Every bay and inlet, beach and park, leafy avenue and bushland reserve is dotted with ever more beautiful houses and gardens, many with box-seat water views of the harbour or Parramatta River.

And that's just the half of it. Head for the northern beaches, stretching from Manly to Palm Beach, and you'll find a dazzling coastline of beaches, cliffs, lakes, bays and headlands that most countries would sell their souls for. All this and more within an hour's drive of the city centre.

We've chosen eight Magic Moments on the north shore and northern beaches but we're sure you'll find many more of your own. All, except Ku-ring-gai Chase, can be reached easily by public transport and make for a wonderful escape from the city. You'll need a car to explore the rugged bushland of Ku-ring-gai.

From ancient Aboriginal rock art to blond-mopped surfers riding the ocean waves, the north shore and northern beaches offer a quintessential slice of Sydney life.

At a Glance

Kirribilli is a five-minute ferry ride from Circular Quay (Wharf 4 or 6). It's the first stop on the north shore train line (Milsons Point Station). A taxi ride from the Quay costs about $10 one-way.

Cremorne Point is a 10-minute ferry ride from Circular Quay (Wharf 4). A taxi ride costs about $15 one-way.

Taronga Zoo is a 12-minute ferry ride from Circular Quay (Wharf 2). A Zoo Pass includes ferry, bus and zoo admission. A taxi ride costs about $20 one-way.

Balmoral is a 20-minute drive from the city or take the ferry from Circular Quay (Wharf 2) to Taronga Park Wharf which is met by bus 238 to Balmoral. There's a weekend ferry service in summer. A taxi ride costs about $20 one-way.

The start of the **Spit to Manly Walk** is a 20-minute drive from the city. Buses 169, 175 and 178 run to Spit Bridge from Wynyard Station. A taxi ride costs about $20 one-way.

Manly is 30 minutes by ferry, 15 minutes by JetCat, from Circular Quay (Wharf 2 or 3). It's a 25-minute drive. A taxi ride costs about $30 one-way.

Ku-ring-gai Chase National Park is a 40-minute drive from the city.

Palm Beach is about an hour's drive from the city. Bus L90 runs from the corner of Pitt and Hay streets in the city. A taxi ride costs about $60 one-way.

For bus, train and ferry information: call (131 500). Taxi fares are metered and depend on the level of traffic. These are approximate fares only. There's a $2 Harbour Bridge toll in each direction.

Shelly Beach.

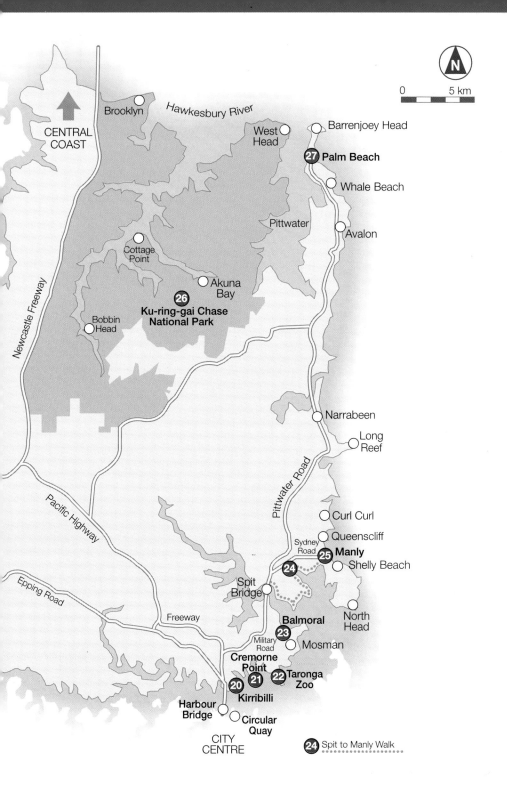

N

0   5 km

Brooklyn

Hawkesbury River

CENTRAL
COAST

West
Head

Barrenjoey Head

27 Palm Beach

Whale Beach

Pittwater

Avalon

Cottage
Point

Akuna
Bay

26
Ku-ring-gai Chase
National Park

Bobbin
Head

Newcastle Freeway

Narrabeen

Long
Reef

Pacific Highway

Pittwater Road

Curl Curl

Queenscliff

Epping Road

Sydney
Road

25 Manly

Shelly Beach

24

Spit
Bridge

Freeway

Balmoral

North
Head

Military
Road

23

Mosman

Cremorne
Point

21   22 Taronga
Zoo

20

Kirribilli

Harbour
Bridge

Circular
Quay

CITY
CENTRE

24 Spit to Manly Walk

Admiralty House.

JEFFREY ST

LUNA PARK

Kirribilli

Few tourists cross the harbour to Kirribilli, yet it's one of Sydney's prettiest suburbs. Perched on a peninsula, opposite the Opera House, Kirribilli boasts one of the best views of the Harbour Bridge and city skyline.

The short ferry ride from Circular Quay is a magic moment in itself, especially if you board one of Hegarty's Ferries' wooden boats, Emerald Star, Leura or Twin Star, which depart from Wharf 6.

The delightful blue-and-white ferries pass under the bridge, stopping at five northside wharfs: McMahons Point, Lavender Bay, Milsons Point, Jeffrey Street and Beulah Street.

Kirribilli was one of the first settlements on Sydney's north shore and is a maze of streets and avenues, a curious mix of accommodation from $4 million mansions to Housing Commission flats.

It's also home to the modest Kirribilli House, the Sydney residence of the Prime Minister, and the grander Admiralty House, Sydney home of the Governor-General and visiting royals. Both houses sit atop Kirribilli Point and are best seen from the water.

Alight at Jeffrey Street Wharf and you can walk up Broughton Street into Kirribilli, stopping in Bradfield Park for the obligatory photo opportunity, one of the best vantage points on the harbour.

The leafy village is a raffish mix of shops, cafes and restaurants, and a pleasant place for a coffee. Continue along Broughton Street and turn right into McDougall Street, lined with jacarandas, where you'll find the pretty Milson Park and Careening Cove.

This was a centre for repairs for Sydney's colonial shipping fleet and a marina is a reminder of its maritime glory days. It's also home to The Ensemble, one of Sydney's best suburban theatres (see Must See).

The most beautiful walk starts from Milsons Point Wharf, under the Harbour Bridge, and leads past the historic Luna Park fun fair to Lavender Bay. Luna Park has been closed for some years – it's being developed into a major new entertainment complex – but the famous smiling face still beams day and night.

Visit on a weekend and you may see bridal couples having their photographs taken in front of the face. Strange but true. The North Sydney swimming pool, close to Milsons Point Wharf, is a great place for a dip (closed for renovations until early 2000).

You can follow the boardwalk past Luna Park, around the yacht-filled Lavender Bay and walk up to Blues Point Road in McMahons Point, a pleasant street of terrace houses and cafes.

Return to the city by train from Milsons Point station (entry via Alfred Street, Milsons Point, or Ennis Road, Kirribilli), or climb the bridge stairs near the station and walk back across the Harbour Bridge to The Rocks.

Directions Kirribilli lies directly across the harbour from the Opera House. Sydney Ferries (131 500) operates services from Wharf 4 at Circular Quay to Milsons Point (for Luna Park). Hegarty's Ferries (9206 1167) operates a private service from Wharf 6 at Circular Quay to Jeffrey Street Wharf (for Kirribilli).

magicmoment

Stopping for the obligatory Me-and-the-Opera House photo in Bradfield Park with its panorama of the Harbour Bridge and city.

mustsee

A play at The Ensemble (9929 0644), one of Sydney's best suburban theatres. The neighbouring Milson Park and Careening Cove are very pretty.

mustdo

The walk along the wooden boardwalk from Milsons Point Wharf, past Luna Park, and around Lavender Bay. It's especially beautiful at sunset.

Cremorne Point

21

magicmoment

Enjoying a picnic at
Cremorne Reserve,
magical at any
time of day.

mustsee

The leafy reserve
at Robertsons
Point with its
whitewashed
lighthouse and
panoramic
harbour views.

mustdo

The delightful
walk around to
Mosman Bay,
stopping to enjoy
the tropical Lex
and Ruby Graham
Gardens.

There are many spectacular views around Sydney Harbour but few come better than the one from Cremorne Point, a narrow peninsula jutting out from the lower north shore. If you're looking for a classic Sydney panorama, complete with harbour, bridge, Opera House and city, this is the place to bring the camera.

The 10-minute ferry ride from Circular Quay is a joy in itself, with lots of photo opportunities from the back of the boat, but the views from Cremorne Point are magnificent. They're even better at weekends when the harbour is filled with yachts, the replica of the Bounty and other harbour cruisers.

Cremorne Point was originally known as Careening Bay. The Sirius, flagship of the First Fleet, was careened (repaired) here in 1789. The Point was gazetted as a reserve in 1833 but almost became a coal mine in the late 1800s when a seam was discovered. Thankfully those plans never eventuated.

Cremorne Point is now a beautiful residential peninsula. Climb the stone steps in front of the wharf and you'll find Robertsons Point, a bushy reserve on the tip of the peninsula leading to a whitewashed lighthouse. A pathway winds through a canopy of trees to the point with panoramic views to Taronga Zoo, Bradleys Head and the central harbour.

Walk back towards the wharf and a paved track will lead you around the peninsula to Cremorne Reserve, a sliver of neatly clipped lawns and foreshore rocks, shaded by palm trees and bordered by expensive apartments, all enjoying panoramic views to the city.

The walkway is a delight, stretching round to Shell Cove. You'll see sleek cruisers and yachts moored here, framed by some of the northside's ritzy harbourside homes on Kurraba Point.

Cremore Reserve is an ideal spot for a picnic – take the steps down to the MacCallum swimming pool to cool off in the heat of summer – and it's a prime viewing location for the city's firework displays.

The highlight of Cremorne Point is the walk around Mosman Bay, on the eastern side of the peninsula, which starts from Robertsons Point and winds past some beautiful ornamental gardens.

The gardens were created by two local residents, the late Lex Graham and his wife Ruby, who have cultivated a tropical Garden of Eden along the foreshore.

The bush-covered bay is filled with yachts at anchor and is a very pretty setting with more glamorous homes hugging the foreshore. You can return to Cremorne Point or continue on the walk to Mosman Wharf for the ferry ride back to the city.

Cremorne Point is compact and very easy to walk around. There are information boards with suggested walking trails and details about the history of the peninsula.

Directions Cremorne Point is a peninsula on Sydney's lower north shore, between Kirribilli and Taronga Zoo. The easiest way to visit it is on a 10-minute ferry ride from Circular Quay (Wharf 4) to Cremorne Wharf (131 500).

Cool off at MacCallum Pool with its stunning harbour views.

Zoo with a view, especially for the giraffes.

Taronga Zoo

Admit it. You want to have your photograph taken with a koala. You want to crouch next to a kangaroo, peer at a possum, and have a good look at a wombat, platypus, dingo, echidna and Tasmanian devil – all those weird and wonderful animals that are only found in Australia. Well, you've come to the right place.

There are two ways of seeing these unique native animals and birds. You can travel the length and breadth of the country for a few months and maybe, just maybe, get a fleeting glimpse of them, or you can take a 12-minute ferry ride from Circular Quay across Sydney Harbour and see them all up close and personal at Taronga Zoo.

One of the world's great animal and bird collections, Taronga is a zoo with a difference.

Perched on Bradleys Head in leafy Mosman, the zoo is a vast complex of spacious animal enclosures weaving their way down the headland like a giant snakes-and-ladders game.

Alligators, elephants, giraffes, gorillas, lions, orang-utans, snow leopards and a white tiger are just some of the dozens of rare and exotic species found in Taronga's tree-shaded compounds.

Then there's the Australian contingent of kangaroos and wallabies, possums and dingos, tree frogs and deadly snakes, saltwater crocodiles and platypus, echidnas and wombats, as well as a vast collection of colourful native birds.

Each enclosure and aviary has been carefully designed to mirror the natural environment of the resident animal or birds, complete with public viewing areas offering clear views of the wildlife without disturbing their daily routines.

It's also a zoo with a view. Stand by the giraffe enclosure or the bird show amphitheatre for terrific panoramas of the city and harbour.

The zoo, opened in 1916, is a wonderful place for children of all ages. The zoo trails are well marked and easy to follow, although you'll need some stamina to walk the entire complex.

There are daily keeper talks, animal and bird shows (the Kodak Free Flight Bird Show is great fun with various birds of prey being put through their paces), guided zoo walks and behind-the-scenes tours. There are also twilight concerts in summer, a "breakfast with the animals" program, and lots of other family entertainment. Check with the zoo information centre for timings.

One of the most popular zoo attractions is the koala enclosure where you can have your picture taken next to the cuddly marsupial. Unlike other wildlife parks, the zoo doesn't allow you to "cuddle" a koala but the Australian Walkabout enclosure offers the chance to get close to the native animals.

Directions Taronga Zoo is on Bradleys Head Road, Mosman, best reached by a delightful 12-minute ferry ride from Wharf 2 at Circular Quay. The zoo (9969 2777) is open daily throughout the year, 9am-5pm, $16 adult, $8.50 child. Sydney Ferries (131 500) offers a Zoo Pass, costing $21 adult, $10.50 child, which includes the ferry ride and zoo admission. www.zoo.nsw.gov.au

magicmoment

Having your picture taken next to a koala. How cute is that?

mustsee

The Kodak Free Flight Bird Show with a black kite, sea eagle, peregrine falcon and black-breasted buzzard among the star attractions.

mustdo

Visit the Australian Walkabout enclosure, where you can get up close and personal with kangaroos and wallabies.

Balmoral

magicmoment

Swimming, sunbathing and relaxing on the calm-water Edwards or Balmoral beaches.

mustsee

The Bathers' Pavilion, now a swish restaurant and cafe (9969 5050), but still providing changing facilities.

mustdo

Join the locals for a twilight stroll along The Esplanade.

This is one of Sydney's best-kept secrets, a gorgeous inner harbour suburb with two beaches, calm-water swimming, a delightful promenade, harbour views, restaurants and cafes, yet few tourists know about it.

Balmoral residents are very protective about their million-dollar turf and probably for good reason. Why tell the world when they can enjoy it all to themselves?

This glamorous beachside community – overlooking Middle Harbour, north of Mosman – may bear the same name as Queen Victoria's favourite castle but it's as far removed from the lochs and glens of Scotland as it's possible to get.

Sydney's Balmoral seems to bask in perennial sunshine with locals and savvy visitors flocking to its twin beaches and leafy parklands. They come to swim and sunbake, catch up for a coffee or a sandwich, lunch or dinner, and take a break from city stress.

It's hard not to relax in Balmoral, with its million-dollar homes, tropical gardens, and leafy avenues cascading down the harbour foreshore to the sparkling water.

A stroll along The Esplanade, a swim on Edwards Beach or Balmoral Beach, and a walk over the tiny bridge onto Rocky Point, which separates the two, will have you in instant holiday mode.

It gets busy at weekends and in the early evening, when locals promenade along The Esplanade for their daily constitution, but during the week you'll pretty much have the place to yourself.

Edwards Beach has a shark net and there's an enclosed pool at the southern end of Balmoral Beach but many people swim in the open water. There are yachts and windsurfers for hire, sandwich bars, and a good fish-and-chip shop (corner of The Esplanade and Raglan Road) if you want a picnic lunch on the beach.

For a classy meal, there are two top-drawer beachside restaurants – the beautiful Bathers' Pavilion to the north, The Watermark to the south – and smaller restaurants across from The Esplanade, all favourite watering holes for Balmoral's well-heeled residents.

The harbour views are delightful with Middle Head to the right, dominated by the HMAS Penguin naval base, Dobroyd Head (part of Sydney Harbour National Park) to the left, and the rugged cliffs of Sydney Heads on the horizon.

There's a relaxed informality about Balmoral. The Romanesque bandstand is a popular venue for weddings and summer performances of Shakespeare plays, and the tree-shaded lawns are ideal for a picnic.

There's even a memorial to Billy, a dearly departed dog and best friend to one of Balmoral's street-sweepers. Sit back and relax, it's that kind of place.

Directions Balmoral is nestled in Middle Harbour, just to the north of Mosman. It's a 20-minute drive from the city (via Military Road, Neutral Bay, Cremorne and Mosman). You can also take a ferry from Wharf 2 at Circular Quay to Taronga Park Wharf which is met by bus 238 which travels to Balmoral. There's a weekend ferry service from Circular Quay but only in summer (131 500).

One of Sydney's most beautiful harbour beaches.

Sydney Harbour from the Spit to Manly Walk.

Spit to Manly Walk

This is one of Sydney Harbour's best scenic walking tracks, winding past modern harbourside homes, ancient Aboriginal sites, native coastal heath, pockets of sub-tropical rainforest, secluded beaches, and lookouts offering truly spectacular views.

There are parts of the track which have changed little since the First Fleet arrived in 1788. Wander through the undergrowth alongside delicate wildflowers, she-oaks and red gums and you can almost feel the spirits of the Kameraigal tribe of Aborigines who once inhabited the area.

The Spit to Manly Walk, or Manly Scenic Walkway as it's sometimes known, is a 10km hike which drops into dense bushland, soars along clifftop escarpments, and winds alongside the harbour foreshore with a picture-postcard array of sights along the way.

The entire walk will take about three to four hours at a leisurely pace but it's also split into shorter, easier trails lasting between 20 and 40 minutes if you only want to do part of it. The joy of the walk is you don't know what's around the next corner and the curiosity factor will likely spur you on the full distance.

You can do the walk in either direction, starting from Spit Bridge (the track starts just north of the bridge; take the first right-hand turn before Avona Crescent) and ending in Manly, or vice versa, although the Spit to Manly direction is probably the best.

Follow the marked trail past Clontarf Beach and along Castle Rock Track, taking time to walk down to the historic Grotto Point Lighthouse, built in 1911 to guide ships into the harbour, then along Arabanoo Walk to Dobroyd Track. This is the most scenic part of the walk with sweeping views over the rugged foreshore and harbour.

Stop at Reef Beach for a refreshing swim, before heading on to the pretty Forty Baskets Beach, North Harbour Reserve at Fairlight, around Fairlight Walk to Manly Cove and the ferry ride back to the city.

It's an uneven track in parts, with some tree roots, rocks and makeshift steps to clamber over, so keep an eye on the footpath. You'll need comfortable walking shoes, a backpack to carry water, sunscreen and a hat. It's also worth taking binoculars for bird-watching if you have them and, of course, your camera.

This is classic Australian bush containing a good deal of wildlife and birdlife – possums, lizards, wattle birds, honey-eaters and rainbow lorikeets – so tread carefully and you might be lucky with a sighting. This is part of Sydney Harbour National Park, so no dogs are allowed.

Directions You can do the Spit to Manly Walk in either direction. Buses 169, 175 and 178 go to Spit Bridge from Wynyard train station, and you can return from Manly by ferry to Circular Quay, or vice versa (131 500). The entire walk is 10km long and takes three to four hours. The Manly Visitor Information Centre (see next page) has an informative map.

magicmoment

Hiking across the windswept bushland of Dobroyd Head with its sweeping views of Sydney Harbour and the Pacific Ocean.

mustsee

Reef Beach, perfect for a refreshing swim.

mustdo

All or part of the walk. It's one of the best scenic harbour trails in Sydney.

Manly

magicmoment

Walking along Marine Parade to Fairy Bower and Shelly Beach from the southern end of Manly Beach. There are two restaurants, a rock pool, stunning views to the northern beaches, and calm-water swimming.

mustsee

The clifftop at North Head offers a dramatic panorama of the Pacific Ocean and Sydney Harbour.

mustdo

A guided tour of the Quarantine Station (9977 6522). Evening "ghost" tours – the place is said to be haunted – are also available (see page 133).

If you're looking for the classic Sydney experience, this is just the ticket. Cross the harbour on the Manly ferry, walk down The Corso to Manly Beach, have a swim in the Pacific Ocean, lunch in one of the beachside cafes, walk around the ocean promenade to Fairy Bower and Shelly Beach, enjoy another dip, walk back to Manly for dinner, and hop on the JetCat back to Circular Quay.

No visit to Sydney would be complete without a trip to Manly, preferably on one of those balmy, cloudless days when the harbour and ocean seem to melt into the sky. Manly has long touted itself as "seven miles from Sydney, a thousand miles from care" and it's no idle boast.

The gateway to Sydney's northern beaches, Manly is a bustling beachside resort enjoying the best of the beach and harbour.

The harbour side is dominated by Manly Wharf with its ferries, JetCats, amusement arcade, restaurants and shops. There's a calm-water beach on either side of the wharf, yachts bob at anchor, and Oceanworld Manly and Manly Art Gallery lie at the western end.

Opposite the wharf entrance is The Corso, a raffish pedestrian mall of tourist shops, restaurants, cafes and ice-cream parlours leading past palm trees and seagulls to the oceanside Manly Beach.

This is classic Sydney, a picture-postcard strip of golden sand, rolling waves, sun-bronzed lifesavers and beautiful bodies, all framed by a paved promenade lined with towering Norfolk pines and crowded with locals taking in the sea air, cycling, roller-blading, waxing their surfboards, or tucking into fish and chips. Were it not for the palm trees and blue sky, this could be a bucket-and-spade English seaside resort. It's busy, brash and spells holiday with a capital H.

It's thought Manly's unusual name sprang from Captain Arthur Phillip's first encounter in 1788 with a group of Aborigines of "manly" physique. It was one of Sydney's first beach resorts to allow daylight swimming and surfing in 1902 and is still a place to show off the bod.

Aside from the beach, there's plenty to see and do. The walk to Fairy Bower and Shelly Beach (see Magic Moment) is beautiful. Take the bus to North Head, stopping at the Quarantine Station for a guided tour (see page 133), or wander the grounds of the beautiful St Patrick's seminary, now a hotel management college, which dominates the Manly skyline.

There are more than 60 restaurants to choose from and a variety of hotels, apartments and guest houses close to the beach if you want to stay longer.

Directions Manly is 30 minutes by ferry, 15 minutes by JetCat from Circular Quay (Wharf 2 or 3). The ferry runs every half-hour, 6am-7.40pm, the JetCat every half-hour to midnight (131 500). Bus 135 runs from Manly Wharf to North Head, St Patrick's and the Quarantine Station. The Manly Visitor Information Centre (9977 1088) is next to Manly's surf beach, open daily, 10am-4pm (except Christmas Day); www.manly.nsw.gov.au

Fish and chips on Manly's bustling Corso.

Savour the tranquillity of Ku-ring-gai Chase National Park.

Ku-ring-gai Chase

This vast expanse of thick bushland, tree-shrouded bays and deep-water inlets, carved over centuries by the relentless flow of the Hawkesbury River, is only 24 kilometres north of Sydney's central business district but it might be a different world.

There's a peace and tranquillity in Ku-ring-gai Chase National Park that 200 years of urban development beyond its borders has failed to disturb. The place is still much like it was when Aborigines lived in its rock shelters, fished in its bays, and hunted animals for food.

Ku-ring-gai is a natural art gallery of rock engravings and paintings, providing a window on the park's ancient history. The "whitefellas" cars and boats may weave through its roads and waterways but the Aboriginal spirit is writ large across this sandstone wilderness.

The name Ku-ring-gai derives from the Garigal Aboriginal clan (Guringai is the name of their language) who inhabited the area for at least 10,000 years and there are many engravings in the soft sandstone rock throughout the park depicting fish, human figures and tools.

You'll need a vehicle and comfortable walking shoes to explore the 15,000 hectares of rugged parkland but the rewards are many. There are magnificent views, especially from the lookout at West Head, over the mouth of the Hawkesbury, Broken Bay and Central Coast, Lion Island, the beautiful Pittwater and Palm Beach peninsula.

There are more than 45 walking tracks – West Head is a maze of trails – leading to secluded beaches, waterfalls, stands of wildflowers, and an intricate shoreline which is the very essence of Aboriginal Dreamtime stories.

There's also an abundance of wildlife and birdlife. Call by the National Parks and Wildlife Service's Kalkari Visitor Centre (Ku-ring-gai Chase Road, Mt Colah) and you can see kangaroos and emus wandering around the undergrowth. Explore deeper into the park and you may get a fleeting glimpse of wallabies, possums, lizards and lyre birds.

Trails range from the short Discovery Track (with wheelchair access) from the visitor centre to day-long bushwalks. On West Head (the best access is from Mona Vale Road at Terrey Hills) the 3.5km Garigal Aboriginal Heritage Walk leads to The Red Hand Cave rock art site.

Akuna Bay, in the delightful Coal and Candle Creek, has a marina, and the waterside Cottage Point and Bobbin Head are also very pretty.

If you have time, there's a pleasant four-hour weekday ferry service from Brooklyn, just to the north of the park, to the remote communities of the Hawkesbury River. It's called Australia's Last Riverboat Postman and costs $30 an adult, bookings essential (9985 7566).

Directions The best way to explore Ku-ring-gai Chase National Park is by car. It's a 40-minute drive north of the city centre, via the Pacific Highway and Newcastle Freeway, and is open daily, sunrise to sunset, $9 a vehicle a day. The Kalkari Visitor Centre (9457 9853) is on Ku-ring-gai Chase Road, Mt Colah, open daily, 9am-5pm.

26

magicmoment

Standing on West Head and looking across Pittwater to Palm Beach and Barrenjoey Lighthouse.

mustsee

The beautiful marina at Akuna Bay and the bush-covered Coal and Candle Creek.

mustdo

A walk to Aboriginal rock art sites on The Basin Track, Elvina Track and Red Hand Track, all accessible from West Head Road.

Palm Beach

27

magicmoment

Taking the delightful 20-minute ferry ride from Palm Beach Wharf across Pittwater to The Basin, $7 return, Palm Beach Ferries (9918 2747).

mustsee

The beautiful (and not-so-beautiful) bodies sunning themselves on Palm Beach.

mustdo

The Basin Trail, leading to a collection of Aboriginal rock carvings. It's an uphill 30-minute walk (steep at the start) but the carvings are worth the effort.

Palm Beach is the playground of Sydney's rich and famous, the most northerly of the northern beaches. This is where the big end of town hangs out, rubs Gucci T-shirts and Prada sandshoes, tops up the tan, lunches until dinner, and swaps deliciously scandalous society gossip.

The Malibu of Sydney, Palm Beach is the weekend escape and holiday retreat of millionaires and media moguls, film stars and TV actors, lawyers and financiers, and the A-list social set for whom life really is a beach. All of which makes this chi-chi suburb, straddling a peninsula separating Pittwater and the Pacific Ocean, a great place to visit.

Perched on stilts, balancing on cliffsides, and leaping from the pages of *Architectural Digest*, these elegant homes and gardens scream out to be looked at.

It's all very tasteful, of course, and shrouded in a mass of tropical foliage but you can't help but wonder where all the money comes from. No matter. The beach is free, the cafes serve decent fare, and the welcome mat is out for everyone.

The beach, a near-perfect crescent of golden sand, is a mecca for surfers and swimmers, although it's prone to dangerous tides, currents and rips. The north and south ends are patrolled at weekends and remember, always swim between the flags.

Palm Beach has a public golf course and excellent restaurants – Beach Road (9974 1159) and the clifftop Jonahs (9974 5599) at nearby Whale Beach are recommended – while the cafes

on The Strand, a location for *Home and Away*, one of Australia's popular TV soap operas, are very pleasant.

If you're feeling energetic, the peninsula rises to a headland and Barrenjoey Lighthouse. It's quite a climb but the views of the ocean, Broken Bay and Pittwater are breathtaking.

A wonderful side-trip is the ferry ride from Palm Beach Wharf, on the west side of the peninsula, across Pittwater to The Basin at the foot of Ku-ring-gai National Park (see Magic Moment).

The old ferry boat, Myra, stops at four beach locations but most people hop off at The Basin where you can swim in a lagoon, picnic and fire up a barbecue. There's also a campsite if you want to stay longer but you'll have to book in advance through the National Parks and Wildlife Service (9972 7378).

The Basin Trail leads into the national park to an impressive collection of Aboriginal rock carvings. It's an uphill 30-minute walk (quite steep at the start) but the headland views and ancient rock carvings, many faint but easily discernible, are well worth the effort.

Directions Palm Beach is about an hour's drive from the city centre. Bus L90 runs from the corner of Pitt and Hay streets in the city every half-hour (131 500). If you want to visit Palm Beach in style, Sydney Harbour Seaplanes (1800 803 558) offers flights to Pittwater and lunch at a Palm Beach restaurant for $195 a person (minimum four people).

Lifestyles of the rich and famous in ritzy Palm Beach.

Eastern Suburbs

City centre

I n a city as beautiful as Sydney, it's no surprise to find deep-seated rivalries and suburban loyalties bubbling just below the surface. Just as north shore residents would barely dream of crossing the Harbour Bridge and heading east, so people in the eastern suburbs positively shiver at the thought of heading north. Why bother when everything you need and want is right here on your doorstep?

Such is life in Sydney's east, a collection of silvertail suburbs such as Bellevue Hill and Vaucluse rubbing Chanel-clad shoulders with trendy Paddington, raffish Bondi, and the more family-oriented Coogee and Bronte, which seem to have it all.

Like the north shore and northern beaches, the eastern suburbs are blessed with great natural beauty and dazzling views to the city, harbour and ocean. The harbour foreshore is a chain of beautiful bays, marinas, beaches, parks and headlands, stretching from Elizabeth Bay to Watsons Bay on South Head.

The ocean coastline, extending from South Head to Coogee and on to Botany Bay, is a swathe of craggy cliffs, covered with houses and apartments, parklands and walking trails, and dipping down to beaches and bays which are perfect for a swim on a hot summer's day.

The east's multicultural mix is never more evident than in the myriad restaurants and cafes, especially in Paddington, Bondi and Coogee, and you'll never be far from a decent cup of coffee. Sydney serves up a mean macchiato, so sit back, relax and watch the passing parade.

All our Magic Moments are within easy reach of the city by public transport and the blue Bondi & Bay Explorer Bus (see page 141).

At a Glance

Paddington is a 10-minute drive from the city centre. Bus 389 runs from Circular Quay and winds through the streets of Paddington. A taxi ride from the Quay costs about $10 one-way.

Double Bay is a 15-minute drive from the city. Buses 323, 324 and 325 run from Circular Quay; there's also a daily ferry service from the Quay (Wharf 4). A taxi ride costs about $15 one-way.

Nielsen Park is a 20-minute drive from the city. Bus 325 runs from Circular Quay. A taxi ride costs about $20 one-way.

Watsons Bay is a 25-minute drive from the city. Buses 324 and 325 and a ferry service runs from Circular Quay (Wharf 4). A taxi ride costs about $25 one-way.

Bondi is a 25-minute drive from the city. Buses 380, 382 and 389 run from Circular Quay. Trains run from Central Station to Bondi Junction, then take bus 380 or 389. A taxi ride costs about $25 one-way.

Coogee is a 25-minute drive from the city centre. Bus 373 runs from Circular Quay; there is no train service. A taxi ride costs about $25 one-way.

Royal Randwick is a 15-minute drive from the city. On race days, shuttle buses run from Central. A taxi ride costs about $20 one-way.

Sydney Cricket Ground and **Sydney Football Stadium** are a 10-minute drive from the city. Bus 392 runs from Circular Quay, 393 from Central. A taxi ride costs about $15 one-way.

For bus, train and ferry information: call (131 500). Taxi fares are metered and depend on the level of traffic. These are approximate fares only.

Doyle's at Watsons Bay.

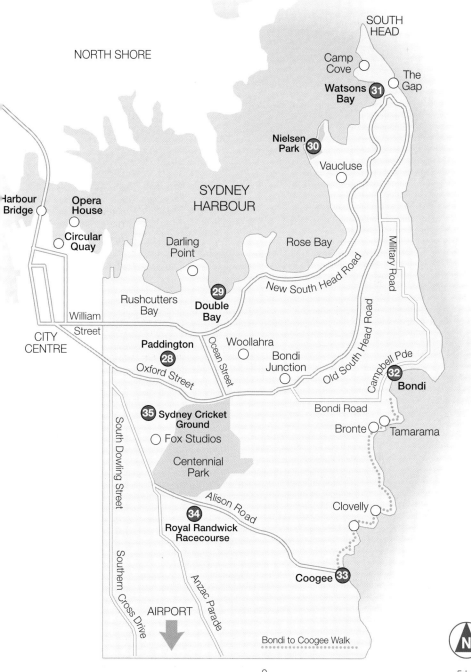

NORTH SHORE

SOUTH HEAD

Camp Cove

The Gap

Watsons **31** Bay

Nielsen Park **30**

Vaucluse

SYDNEY HARBOUR

Harbour Bridge

Opera House

Circular Quay

Darling Point

Rose Bay

New South Head Road

Military Road

Rushcutters Bay

Double Bay **29**

CITY CENTRE

William Street

Paddington **28**

Oxford Street

Ocean Street

Woollahra

Bondi Junction

Old South Head Road

Campbell Pde

Bondi **32**

Bondi Road

Bronte

Tamarama

Sydney Cricket Ground **35**

Fox Studios

South Dowling Street

Centennial Park

Alison Road

Clovelly

Royal Randwick Racecourse **34**

Southern Cross Drive

Anzac Parade

AIRPORT

Coogee **33**

Bondi to Coogee Walk

0   5 km

N

Paddington terrace.

Paddington

There was a time when you couldn't raise a cheer for Paddington. From working-class village to bohemian rhapsody and then inner-city slum, this historic enclave of terrace houses and leafy streets has come good again in spectacular fashion.

One of Sydney's trendiest suburbs, centred on Oxford Street, Paddington enjoys a village atmosphere with pubs, restaurants, antique stores and art galleries, all within sight of the city skyscrapers.

Paddington's hallmark is its terrace houses, row upon row of historic Victorian homes, built in the late 1800s, decorated with delicate wrought-iron lace balconies, and framed by tropical foliage and stately trees. A very pleasant morning or afternoon can be spent wandering the maze of streets and avenues, looking at the elegant homes, browsing in the specialty shops, having lunch or cocktails at one of the historic pubs, and shopping in the groovy fashion and homewear stores of Oxford Street.

There is some exceptional architecture in Paddington – the convict-built sandstone Victoria Barracks (1841), which is still used by the Australian Army and is open for inspection; the beautiful Georgian-style Juniper Hall, and the grandiose Paddington Town Hall are all on Oxford Street – but the terrace houses and lace ironwork verandahs are the signature attraction. You can find them in any of the streets leading off Oxford Street, although the cluster around William, Hopetoun, Cascade, Elizabeth streets and the tree-shaded Paddington Street are among the best.

The pretty Glenmore Road snakes through Paddington and leads to Five Ways, an intersection with five roads running off it, which is home to the historic Royal Hotel, restaurants, cafes and local shops.

Neighbouring Woollahra, another of Sydney's blue-ribbon suburbs, has some of the best antique stores and art galleries in Sydney. The stores in Queen Street, Woollahra, and the Woollahra Antiques Centre at 160 Oxford Street are especially good.

If you have a car, the tree-lined streets and historic homes of Woollahra along Queen, Moncur, Ocean and adjoining streets are beautiful and the glorious 220-hectare expanse of Centennial Park is just across Oxford Street. It's ideal for walking, cycling, horse-riding or a picnic.

Another Sydney institution is Paddington Markets, a colourful and lively bazaar every Saturday morning (see Must See), selling clothes, jewellery, pottery, CDs, and quality arts and crafts. There are fortune-tellers, masseurs, entertainers and all manner of bargains.

There's still a faintly bohemian air about Paddington, despite the steady influx of trendy fashion stores and yuppie residents, but the atmosphere is decidedly cosmopolitan. Grab a cafe latte at an Oxford Street cafe and watch Sydney's beau monde pass by.

Directions Paddington lies to the east of the city centre, beyond Darlinghurst. The main access is via Oxford Street, although bus 389 from Circular Quay winds through Paddington streets, Five Ways and Queen Street, Woollahra (131 500). The Army Museum at Victoria Barracks, Oxford Street (9339 3000), is open on Sunday, 10am-3pm; there's a guided tour and band recital every Thursday at 10am, entry free.

magicmoment

Exploring the maze of Paddington streets with their terrace houses and delicate lace ironwork verandahs.

mustsee

The colourful Paddington Markets, on the corner of Oxford and Newcombe streets, every Saturday, 10am-4pm.

mustdo

Lunch or cocktails at the Royal Hotel, 237 Glenmore Road (9331 2604), a magnet for the Paddington and Woollahra set.

Double Bay

magicmoment

Strolling the ritzy streets and designer stores of Double Bay and watching the beautiful people at play.

mustsee

The pretty wharf and twin beaches next to the NSW 18' Sailing Club at the harbour end of Bay Street.

mustdo

Lunch or coffee at The Cosmopolitan, Knox Street (9326 2334), the place to see and be seen.

You only have to wander down Cross Street, in the heart of Double Bay, to see why this glamorous little suburb is nicknamed Double Pay.

Gleaming Rolls-Royces, BMWs and racy sports cars are parked alongside ritzy boutiques and cafes while beautiful people sashay along the pavement trying to look, well, beautiful.

This is Sydney's Rodeo Drive, a platinum-edged enclave with a price tag to match. You can shop for the best designer goods and most fashionable designer clothes but you'd better make sure your credit card is up to the challenge.

Double Bay is the serious money end of town with enough ready cash to bankroll a minor potentate. The women come with big hair, Grace Kelly sunglasses, Chanel handbags and an attitude that's as sharp as their stilettos. The men are finely chiselled and thoroughly tanned, the children are neatly groomed and perfectly mannered, and even the dogs seem to walk with a swagger.

It's an episode of *The Nanny*, an edition of *Hello!*, and a scene from *Pretty Woman* all rolled into one, with a spectacular harbourside setting that money just can't buy.

It's home to one of Sydney's luxury hotels, the Ritz-Carlton Double Bay, some of the city's leading fashion, homeware, antiques and jewellery stores, art galleries and gift shops, and a swag of restaurants where people-watching is top of the menu but it also has a casual atmosphere which makes for a very pleasant excursion.

Double Bay is a tiny suburb, bordered by Darling Point, Edgecliff, Bellevue Hill and the twin beaches which lend the bay its name. If you're driving from the city, the best route is via William Street and New South Head Road, turning into Double Bay at Ocean Avenue, Knox Street or Cross Street.

There's a cute little row of gabled shops in Transvaal Street, just off Cross Street, and the stores along Bay Street are particularly good. There are sales twice a year in summer and winter (yes, even in Double Bay), so you may even score a bargain of sorts.

Watching the locals at work and play is almost a sport in Double Bay and the legendary Cosmopolitan cafe and restaurant in Knox Street is the ideal vantage point. The Ritz-Carlton Hotel in Cross Street is also a pleasant place for afternoon tea and cocktails.

Wander to the harbour end of Bay Street where you'll find a park, wharf, sailing club and the beach. The water's a little murky for swimming but it's a pleasant place for a picnic and the credit card will, no doubt, feel a lot happier too.

Directions Double Bay is a 15-minute drive east of the city centre along New South Head Road. Buses 323, 324 and 325 run from Circular Quay; there's also a daily ferry service from Wharf 4 at the Quay (131 500). It's stop 6 on the blue Bondi & Bay Explorer bus.

Give the credit card a workout in Double Bay.

Vaucluse House and Shark Beach.

Nielsen Park

Sydney is blessed with beautiful parks but this is one of the best. Nestled on the harbour side of South Head, between Hermit Bay and Vaucluse Bay, Nielsen Park is a popular picnic and swimming spot.

The delighful parkland, part of Sydney Harbour National Park, offers beautiful foreshore walks, panoramic views of the harbour, a pleasant beach and a fine restaurant overlooking Shark Beach.

It's popular in summer and at weekends, when crowds flock to the calm-water beach, but visit Nielsen Park during the week and you'll pretty much have the place to yourself.

Enter the park from Greycliffe Avenue, Vaucluse, where it's a short walk past tree-shaded lawns to the water.

Shark Beach is netted, ideal for children, and offers beautiful views to Bradleys Head and Middle Head across the harbour. Just up from the beach is Nielsen Park Kiosk (see Must Do), built in 1914 in the grounds of historic Greycliffe House, now used as a National Parks and Wildlife Service office.

The Hermitage Foreshore, a 1.5km walking trail, leads from the western end of the beach past Milk Beach, Hermit Point and Queens Beach to Rose Bay and offers expansive views of the harbour. You can also walk up to Vaucluse Point from the eastern end of the beach.

Further along Wentworth Road is Vaucluse House, one of Sydney's most beautiful historic houses. While the castellated sandstone house is best known as the home of explorer William Charles Wentworth, who bought the property in 1827, it was actually built 24 years earlier as a small stone cottage for an Irish knight, Sir Henry Brown Hayes.

It was just as well the house was extended and remodelled because Wentworth and his wife Sarah, a former convict's daughter who proved to be an astute manager of the estate, proceeded to fill the house with 10 children.

Today, Vaucluse House lies at the heart of Sydney's colonial history. The wonderful grounds and gardens extend over 10 hectares of the original estate, which once amounted to 206 hectares, and careful research has helped restore the original gardens and carriageways. There's also a pleasant tearoom in the grounds.

It's the oldest house museum in Australia and furnished to the era of the Wentworth family's occupation from 1827. It was bought by the State Government in 1910, opened to the public in 1924, and is now part of the Historic Houses Trust of New South Wales (see page 132).

Directions Nielsen Park lies on the harbour side of South Head, beyond Rose Bay. From the city, drive east along William Street and New South Head Road and turn left into Vaucluse Road, just after the Sacred Heart Convent (stop here for a panoramic harbour view). Nielsen Park is stop 9 on the blue Bondi & Bay Explorer bus; bus 325 from Circular Quay stops at Vaucluse House (9388 7922), open Tuesday to Sunday, 10am-4.30pm (except Good Friday and Christmas Day), $6 adult.

magicmoment

Relaxing on Shark Beach (shark in name only!) with its delightful views of the harbour.

mustsee

Vaucluse House, the oldest house museum in Australia, built in 1827.

mustdo

Lunch at Nielsen Park Kiosk (9337 1574), pricey but good; open daily, except Monday. There's also a cafe and takeaway service in summer.

Watsons Bay

(31)

magicmoment

A long, long lunch at Doyle's on the Beach (9337 2007). Seafood and stunning harbour views washed down with a chilled bottle of chardonnay. The classic Sydney experience.

mustsee

The rugged cliffs at Gap Bluff plunging into the foaming surf of the Pacific Ocean.

mustdo

The beautiful walk from Camp Cove, past Lady Jane Beach, to Hornby Lighthouse at South Head.

There are certain things you must do on a visit to Sydney: a performance at the Opera House, a harbour cruise, a ride on the Manly ferry, a swim at Bondi Beach. There's one other treat to add to the list – lunch or dinner at Doyle's on the Beach at Watsons Bay.

This legendary seafood restaurant, with its wonderful views of the harbour, is the essence of Sydney. Ask for a courtyard table, order oysters, lobster and barramundi, crack open a bottle of chardonnay and toast your good fortune.

Owned and operated since 1885 by one of Sydney's great seafood and restaurant dynasties, Doyle's is just one of many treats at Watsons Bay, perched almost on the tip of South Head.

Billed as the oldest fishing village in Australia (the First Fleet set up tents at Camp Cove in 1788 after arriving from Botany Bay), it's a picture-postcard collection of fishermen's cottages, parklands, restaurants, cafes and dramatic coastal walks.

The main activity is centred on Watsons Bay beach, scattered with upturned rowing boats and framed by Doyle's, the public wharf and the lively Watsons Bay Hotel with its pleasant waterfront beer garden.

You can swim at the beach or an enclosed pool at the southern end of the beach, and buy fish and chips at the wharf or pub if you don't want to eat at the restaurant.

Work up an appetite with a walk along Cliff Street to Camp Cove and then take the harbour foreshore walk, past Lady Jane Beach (one of Sydney's handful of nudist beaches) to the colourful Hornby Lighthouse on South Head.

The lighthouse, painted with vivid red and white stripes to distinguish it from Macquarie Lighthouse south of Dunbar Head, was built after a migrant ship, the Dunbar, was wrecked at Gap Bluff in 1857. It remains Sydney's worst maritime tragedy with all but one of the 122 people on board perishing in the tragedy.

There are information boards explaining the history of the lighthouse and fortifications. HMAS Watson military reserve covers much of the headland but the walk offers wonderful views of the harbour and ocean waves crashing against South Head.

The most dramatic views are at Gap Bluff, where a boardwalk leads along the clifftop of The Gap Park and Sydney Harbour National Park (access via steps in Military Road).

The Gap is a deep scar in the cliff and a favourite suicide spot, all the more poignant given the beautiful setting, but Watsons Bay isn't for dark thoughts. Simply relax and enjoy the views.

Directions Watsons Bay lies on South Head. By car, drive east from the city along William Street, New South Head Road and Hopetoun Avenue. Watsons Bay and The Gap are stops 10 and 11 on the blue Bondi & Bay Explorer bus. Buses 324 and 325 operate from Circular Quay; there's also a regular ferry service from Wharf 4 at the Quay (131 500).

Treat yourself to lunch at Doyle's on the Beach.

Bondi Beach, an Aussie icon.

Bondi

Australia's most famous beach barely needs an explanation, yet the reality is not as some people imagine. Classic photographs of sun-bronzed bodies lying on golden sand and blond-mopped surfers riding the waves give the impression that Bondi stretches as far as the imagination but it's actually quite a modest city beach.

It's wide and curved, rather than long and straight, with an uninspiring backdrop of red-brick and colour-washed apartments, hotels, shops and restaurants cluttered around the bay.

Take away the sun and the surf and you could be in a typical English seaside resort. Even the names of the streets – Queen Elizabeth Drive, Ramsgate Avenue, Brighton Boulevard and Hastings Parade – lend the place a decidedly British air but that's where the similarities end. When the sun shines, a swell is running and the air smells sweet with sea salt and coconut oil, you can rest assured that Bondi ain't Blackpool.

In the height of summer, this is quintessential Australia, the beach covered with tanned bodies, colourful sun umbrellas, bronzed lifesavers – their distinctive red and yellow outfits matching the flags which tell people where they can swim – and waves filled with swimmers and surfers.

The beachside promenade is a parade of joggers and roller-bladers while the hotels, restaurants and cafes of Campbell Parade, rising to Ben Buckler headland to the north and Mackenzies Point to the south, are a constant hive of activity.

A magnet for backpackers and tourists in search of a good time, Bondi has long suffered from a seedy image, not helped by litter, graffiti and rowdy Christmas and New Year's Eve celebrations, but Sydney's sacred beach is making determined efforts to clean up its act.

Campbell Parade now has some of the best beachside cafes and restaurants in Sydney, such as Bondi Tratt and Hugo's at the southern end, Raw Bar and Sean's Panorama at the northern end.

New apartments are springing up and yuppies are moving in. Old Bondi hands say the place is losing its essential character, but it will always have a slightly raffish, devil-may-care atmosphere but with better places to stay, eat and drink.

There are two surf clubs, an imposing beach pavilion (with a cafe, exhibition rooms and changing facilities), and the coastal walk from Bondi to Tamarama and Bronte (which starts from the southern end of Campbell Parade beside the Bondi Icebergs rock pool) is a delight (see page 135). When all is said and done, Bondi is the beach – an Aussie icon at the core of Sydney life.

Directions Bondi Beach is a 25-minute drive from the city centre, along Oxford Street, Syd Einfeld Drive and Bondi Road. Buses 380, 382 and 389 run from Circular Quay to Bondi Beach or you can take the train from Central to Bondi Junction and bus 380 or 389 to Bondi Beach (131 500). It's stop 12 on the blue Bondi & Bay Explorer bus.

magicmoment
What can we say? Sun, sand, surf and more bronzed bodies than you could poke a bikini at on Australia's most famous beach.

mustsee
Bondi's beautiful people in the groovy restaurants and cafes along Campbell Parade.

mustdo
The 40-minute clifftop walk from Bondi to Tamarama and Bronte with spectacular views of the coastline and Pacific Ocean.

Coogee

magicmoment

Tucking into a picnic of prawns and champagne at Dunningham Reserve on the northern headland of Coogee Beach. The lights of the bay are especially pretty in the evening.

mustsee

The historic Wylie's Baths, next to Grant Reserve on the southern headland of the beach.

mustdo

The coastal walk north from Coogee Beach to Gordons Bay, Clovelly, and on to Bronte, Tamarama and Bondi.

Like Bondi, Coogee is enjoying a resurgence in its fortunes and has become a very desirable place to live. It's not as groovy or as busy as Bondi but it has been smartened up considerably and gained an array of new beachside restaurants and cafes.

Coogee also has some fine hotels and backpacker accommodation which are attracting a new clientele. Instead of staying in the city centre and visiting the beach, many Sydney visitors are basing themselves in Coogee, enjoying its relaxed holiday atmosphere, and making day trips into the city.

Coogee Beach is not unlike Bondi, a pretty crescent of golden sand with a south-easterly aspect, but is smaller and more compact. It's also a flat-water beach, which doesn't attract the huge waves of Bondi, so it's popular with families and casual swimmers.

The redevelopment of Coogee has given it a very smart paved promenade which follows the curve of the beach and is a magnet for joggers, roller-bladers and people enjoying a beachside stroll.

Once a sedate seaside community (complete with a Blackpool-style pier, long since disappeared), Coogee has been given a contemporary makeover and now has some upmarket restaurants, cafes and bars.

Barzura in Carr Street, on the southern headland, has a delightful outlook across the bay and serves decent food, although you can pretty much take your pick of places to eat and drink.

If you don't want to swim in the surf, there are four pools: the sheltered and popular Giles Gym at the northern end of the beach, one in front of the surf club at the southern end, the Women's Pool (women and children only) just around the southern headland, and the historic Wylie's Baths, a little further along Grant Reserve.

The coastal track from Bondi to Tamarama and Bronte extends on to Coogee, although this would take about two hours to walk.

Another option is to start the walk from the north end of Coogee Beach, following Dunningham Reserve around Gordons Bay and Clovelly Bay. The Bondi-Coogee coastal walk is popular at weekends, so it's probably best done during the week.

If you're a keen diver or snorkeller, Gordons Bay has a unique underwater nature trail. The narrow rocky inlet of Clovelly Bay is also good for swimming and snorkelling.

The main Coogee Bay Road, which runs directly to the beach, is a bustling strip of restaurants, cafes, bars and shops, and the Coogee Bay Hotel, on the corner of Arden Street, is a loud and lively watering hole.

Directions Coogee is south of Bondi, about 25 minutes' drive from the city centre, via Anzac Parade, Alison Road, Belmore Road and Coogee Bay Road. Bus 373 runs from Circular Quay to Coogee (131 500). It's stop 14 on the blue Bondi & Bay Explorer bus. There is no train service to Coogee. The green and yellow Airport Express bus service (route 351) also runs between Bondi, Coogee and Sydney Airport.

Coogee offers a relaxed holiday atmosphere.

Royal Randwick

In a city where horse-racing is a passion rather than a sport, it's no surprise to find a major racetrack within galloping distance of the central business district. Royal Randwick has been home to the sport of kings since 1860 and is one of Sydney's major sporting and social venues.

Every race day, thousands of punters head for the hallowed turf of Randwick, hoping this will be their lucky day. It's a lively and colourful racetrack, echoing to the sounds of bookmakers, race callers and crowds urging their horses past the winning post.

Five kilometres to the south-east of the city centre, Randwick boasts a year-round racing calendar. It's also home to the Australian Jockey Club (AJC), the largest racing club in New South Wales which conducts about 60 race meetings annually at Randwick and Warwick Farm, in south-western Sydney.

Horses have been a part of Australian life since the arrival of the First Fleet in 1788. While the history books differ on the fleet's animal cargo, the diaries of Philip Gidley King, a second lieutenant on HMS Sirius and later governor of New South Wales, contend there were two stallions and four mares on board.

By 1798, the colonial stables had grown to 44 stallions and 43 mares, and a year later the blood stallion Rockingham arrived from South Africa, marking the beginning of Australia's thoroughbred industry.

The first official race meeting was held in Sydney's Hyde Park in 1810. The sport moved to Randwick, then known as the Sandy Course, in 1833 for five years when the track was abandoned in favour of Homebush.

The AJC was formed in 1842, moved back to Randwick in 1860, and the racecourse has been the club headquarters ever since.

Today Randwick is the venue for many of Australia's major races, especially during the popular autumn and spring carnivals, with the highlight being the four-day AJC Autumn Carnival of Champions at Easter. The two feature events, the AJC Derby and Doncaster Handicap, carry $2 million and $2.5 million in prize-money respectively.

Australia's annual prize-money, the highest in the world outside the United States and Japan, amounts to almost $260 million. Each year 32,000 racehorses compete in 23,000 races over 3,200 race meetings nationwide for a share in the purse and Royal Randwick is at the heart of the action.

There's a range of restaurants and bars, and a bevy of bookmakers standing by to take your money. The major carnival races attract a social crowd, when the fashions are almost as important as the fillies, but a day at the races at Randwick is fun at any time of the year.

Directions Royal Randwick Racecourse is in Alison Road, Randwick. On race days, shuttle buses operate from Chalmers Street, on the east side of Central train station, direct to the racecourse (131 500). It's stop 15 on the blue Bondi & Bay Explorer bus. Australian Jockey Club (9663 8400); www.ajc.org.au

magicmoment

Picking a winner!

mustsee

The four-day AJC Autumn Carnival of Champions at Easter.

mustdo

Attend a race meet. Individual race day information (9663 8400).

Sydney Cricket Ground

magicmoment

Watching the
Aussies thrash the
Poms in a Test
or one-day
international, a
magic moment
all its own.

mustsee

A cricket or rugby
match: Sydney
Cricket Ground
(1900 963 132);
Sydney Football
Stadium
(1900 963 133).

mustdo

The Sportspace
Tour (see
Directions).

If cricket is a religion, and there are many in Australia who believe it is, the Sydney Cricket Ground is the Holy Grail. This hallowed turf, the battleground for so many glorious victories and painful defeats, is as close to a sporting sacred site as you'll find.

Bradman, Sobers, Botham, Border, Lara and Warne, the names of the cricket greats who've graced this historic stadium roll off the tongue like leather off willow.

The first recorded match at the cricket ground was a club fixture played in 1854 and the stadium has been at the heart of Australia's sporting heritage ever since.

There's a magic about the Sydney Cricket Ground, four kilometres south-east of the city centre at Moore Park, even when it's empty. The great stands, Churchill, Bradman, Brewongle, O'Reilly and the Members' Pavilion, seem to whisper tales of heroic contests and sporting battles won and lost.

When the stadium is full and 50,000 people are cheering every ball and wicket, it's the stuff of sporting legend. Whether it's a Test (usually in early January) or one-day international (December to February), a session at the Sydney Cricket Ground is a magic moment all its own.

It also doubles as the Sydney venue for Australian Football, or Aussie Rules (March to September), and is home to the Sydney Swans.

For rugby fans, nirvana is next door. The Sydney Football Stadium, opened in 1988 as part of the Bicentennial celebrations, hosts major rugby league, rugby union and soccer games and occupies a similar, if slightly less sacred place among Sydney's sporting trophies.

Both grounds are also venues for major entertainment events, such as rock concerts and outdoor operas.

The cricket season runs from October to March and rugby season from March to September. Throughout the year (except on match days and public holidays) you can book a Sportspace Tour and enjoy a behind-the-scenes look at how both stadiums work.

The interactive tour includes the players' dressing rooms, security control room, private boxes, exclusive Members' Pavilion, the Members' Bar, stadium tunnels and a walk beside the hallowed turfs. There are audio visual displays, colourful characters and lots of sporting memorabilia.

If you want tickets to a game or event, check the entertainment and sports pages of Sydney's daily newspapers and call Ticketek (9266 4800). Most major games and events sell out ahead of time, so you're advised to book in advance.

Directions The Sydney Cricket Ground and Sydney Football Stadium are at Moore Park, about four kilometres south-east of the city centre. Bus 392 runs from Circular Quay and bus 393 from Central train station to Anzac Parade, Moore Park (131 500). The stadiums are stop 16 on the blue Bondi & Bay Explorer bus. Sportspace Tours (9380 0383) operate Monday to Saturday, 10am, 1pm and 3pm (excluding match days and public holidays), $18 adult, $12 child/concession, and last about 90 minutes.

Hallowed turf...Sydney Cricket Ground (above) and Sydney Football Stadium.

Western Sydney

City centre

You won't have to spend long in Sydney to realise there's a cultural gulf of Olympic proportions between the west and the rest of the city. Hang around the eastern, northern and southern suburbs for a few days and you'll find an almost sneering attitude to anyone living west of Strathfield.

Known disparagingly as "westies", the people of the western suburbs are baited by their city slicker cousins (most of whom have never been "out west" in their lives) for living far from the action, enjoying few of the attractions and possessing a fraction of their sophistication.

Such intra-urban rivalry should be dismissed out of hand. The harbour, bridge and Opera House may be the cultural heart of Sydney but the geographic and demographic centre is 24 kilometres to the west in Parramatta.

Wedged between the Blue Mountains and Sydney's central business district, and linked by the Parramatta River, this thriving city is the capital of western Sydney and the centre of a massive population base.

It also lies at the core of Australia's history – first as an important Aboriginal site and later as the second white settlement, founded nine months after the arrival of the First Fleet in 1788 – and has some fine examples of Sydney's early colonial architecture.

The west will also play host to the Sydney 2000 Olympic and Paralympic Games, centred on Olympic Park at Homebush Bay, for two months in September and October 2000.

Add other Magic Moments like historic Balmain, in Sydney's inner west, and you'd do as well to ignore the city rivalry and enjoy the west for what it really is.

At a Glance

Balmain lies on a peninsula to the west of the Harbour Bridge. It's a 10-minute ferry ride from Wharf 5 at Circular Quay to Balmain East Wharf (Darling Street). Bus 442 runs from Town Hall; there is no train service to Balmain. A taxi ride from the city centre costs about $20 one-way.

The easiest way to reach **Homebush Bay and the Olympic site** is by train from Central to Lidcombe, then board the Olympic Park Sprint train which runs daily every 10 minutes from 7am to 11.30pm. There are also daily train services from Central via Strathfield and a RiverCat service from Wharf 5 at Circular Quay to Homebush Bay Wharf. Extra services operate during special events and the Olympics. An Explorer Bus tours Olympic Park daily every 20 minutes, 9.30am-3pm (except public holidays), $10 adult. There are also guided walking tours. The **Homebush Bay Information Centre** (9714 7888) is open daily, 9am-5pm. A taxi ride from Sydney CBD costs about $30 one-way.

Parramatta can be reached by RiverCat from Wharf 5 at Circular Quay. There are regular daily services; the journey takes about an hour. It's then a five-minute walk from Charles Street Wharf to Parramatta's central business district. **Parramatta Visitors Centre** is at 346 Church Street (9630 3703), 15 minutes' walk from Church Street Wharf, open daily 10am-4pm, stocked with walking maps and historic sites information. A taxi ride from the city centre costs about $40 one-way.

For bus, train and ferry information: call (131 500). Taxi fares are metered and depend on the level of traffic. These are approximate fares only.

The Balmain ferry.

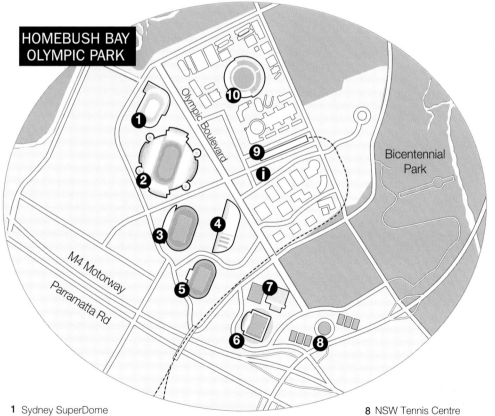

HOMEBUSH BAY OLYMPIC PARK

1 Sydney SuperDome
2 Stadium Australia
3 Athletic Warm-Up Area
4 Sydney International Aquatic Centre
5 Athletic Warm-Up Area
6 State Hockey Centre
7 State Sports Centre
8 NSW Tennis Centre
9 Olympic Park Station
10 Baseball Stadium
i Information Centre

The early morning ferry to Balmain.

Balmain

Balmain is one of the few places where you can get a real sense of Sydney's history. This pretty waterside suburb is steeped in local folklore, has some fine old homes, pubs and public buildings and makes for a very pleasant excursion.

Perched on a peninsula to the west of the Harbour Bridge, in an area defined as the city's inner west, Balmain has been restored to become one of Sydney's trendiest addresses but retains many of the hallmarks of its working-class origins.

The area was named after William Balmain, a surgeon in the First Fleet, and sprang to life in the 1830s as a centre for shipbuilding and maritime services. Thomas Mort built a large dry dock (Mort Bay still bears his name) and other industries such as sawmills, soap factories and coal-mining soon followed.

It was all thirsty work, of course, and by the 1880s Balmain boasted 44 pubs, 21 of which are still serving customers. It's a raffish, almost bohemian suburb, a maze of streets and alleyways offering a window on Sydney's colonial, industrial, commercial and architectural heritage.

The best way to explore Balmain is on foot. Take the ferry to Balmain East Wharf (see Directions) and then walk along Darling Street. Hop on the bus which meets each ferry if you don't want to walk.

The streets either side of Darling Street have some wonderful old sandstone and weatherboard houses, some of them converted former pubs.

Stop by The Watch House (see Must See), a police station and lock-up for Balmain's petty criminals and drunks, for a glimpse of what life was like in the late 1800s in rough and tough Balmain. In 1920, local policeman Ira Gray lived in the house with his wife and 12 of their 14 children.

Further along Darling Street is St Andrew's Church, home to the Balmain Saturday Market (7.30am-4pm). Darling Street then runs into Balmain's town centre, lined with pubs, cafes, restaurants, patisseries, flower stalls, art and craft stores and bookshops.

It's a bustling centre, especially at weekends, but with a pleasant village atmosphere.

Some of the pubs offer live jazz. The historic London Hotel (234 Darling Street) and Exchange Hotel (corner of Beattie and Mullens streets) are great places for an ice-cold beer.

If you have time, walk around Mort Bay and on to Birchgrove, a pretty enclave of waterfront townhouses, especially along Louisa Road. You can take the ferry back to the city from Long Nose Point Wharf.

Another fun tour is to Goat Island, just off Balmain, which has a rich Aboriginal, convict and maritime history. Contact the National Parks and Wildlife Service for details (9247 5033).

Directions Balmain lies on a peninsula to the west of the Harbour Bridge. It's a 10-minute ferry ride from Wharf 5 at Circular Quay to Balmain East Wharf (Darling Street). Bus 442 runs from Town Hall train station (131 500); there is no train service to Balmain.

magicmoment

Enjoying an ice-cold beer on the verandah of the historic and lively London Hotel, 234 Darling Street, when the colourful Balmain Saturday Market is in full swing.

mustsee

The Watch House, 179 Darling Street, built in 1854 as a police station and lock-up, now headquarters for the Balmain Historic Society, open Saturday, noon to 3pm.

mustdo

A tour of Goat Island with its rich Aboriginal, convict and maritime history. Contact the National Parks and Wildlife Service (9247 5033).

Homebush Bay

37

magicmoment

Seeing a sporting or entertainment event in Stadium Australia, the main venue for the Sydney 2000 Olympic and Paralympic Games.

mustsee

Bicentennial Park, 100 hectares of parklands, wetlands and mangroves, cycle paths and walking trails.

mustdo

A bus or guided walking tour of the Olympic site (see Directions).

It seems fitting that Homebush Bay was once an Aboriginal meeting place where ceremonies, contests and demonstrations of skill and strength took place. Centuries later, the site is the venue for the biggest sporting event of all – the Sydney 2000 Olympic and Paralympic Games.

For two heady months in September and October 2000, thousands of the world's greatest athletes and more than a million spectators will descend on Olympic Park, 17 kilometres west of Sydney's central business district, to witness the first Olympic and Paralypmic Games of the new millennium.

Rising like a phoenix from tidal wetlands, mudflats and an industrial site, the Olympic complex is ready to stamp its name in the history books. The 110,000-seat Stadium Australia, the main venue for the event, is the largest arena built for an Olympic Games.

The Sydney 2000 Olympics, from September 15 to October 1, will have more events than any other Games and the pundits are forecasting an unprecedented number of world records.

It's being billed as the "green" Olympics, a Games for the athletes, and the biggest party in Sydney's history.

The centrepiece is the $615 million Stadium Australia, a state-of-the-art complex which will be the venue for the spectacular opening and closing ceremonies and athletics.

Add a 15,000-seat aquatic centre, tennis and hockey arenas, an archery park, the 20,000-seat Sydney SuperDome, Bicentennial Park, Millennium Parklands, an on-site athletes' village, a hotel, restaurants, cafes, golf driving range, train station, visitor centre, and you have the makings of a truly international sporting venue.

The complex is also home to the new Sydney Showground (the old showground at Moore Park is now Fox Studios) which hosts the annual Easter Show (see page 136).

Whether you're visiting Sydney for the 2000 Olympics, Paralympics (October 18-29) or just want to see the Games venues, a visit to Olympic Park is a must.

Olympic tickets went on sale in mid-1999. While most of the major events will be held at Olympic Park, some sports, such as the yachting on Sydney Harbour, will be free and open to all.

Other events will be held at venues around the city, such as Darling Harbour (judo, wrestling, weightlifting, boxing and volleyball) and Bondi (beach volleyball). For full Olympic Games details, access the SOCOG website: www.sydney.olympic.org or call 13 63 63 once you arrive.

Directions: The easiest way to reach Olympic Park is by train from Central to Lidcombe, then board the Olympic Park Sprint train which runs daily every 10 minutes from 7am to 11.30pm. There are also daily train services from Central via Strathfield and a RiverCat service from Wharf 5 at Circular Quay to Homebush Bay Wharf (131 500). Extra services operate during special events and the Olympics. An Explorer Bus tours Olympic Park daily every 20 minutes, 9.30am-3pm (except public holidays), $10 adult. There are also guided walking tours. The Homebush Bay Visitor Centre (9714 7888) is open daily, 9am-5pm.

Stadium Australia in Olympic Park.

New and old ... the RiverCat's progress and Old Government House.

Parramatta

The skyscrapers of Sydney's central business district may seem like the heart of the city but the geographic centre is about 24 kilometres to the west in the historic city of Parramatta.

Founded nine months after the arrival of the First Fleet in 1788, Parramatta has grown into a thriving city and the capital of Sydney's sprawling western suburbs.

Straddling the head of the Parramatta River (Parramatta is an Aboriginal name said to mean "head of the river") the city is a mix of old and new with modern office blocks standing next to some of Australia's oldest buildings.

You could spend several days in Parramatta, exploring the many historic and scenic attractions, and only scratch the surface of its rich heritage.

Barely 12 weeks after arriving in Sydney Cove, Governor Arthur Phillip set off along Parramatta River in search of arable land to sustain the new colony. Within two months a camp was established and by the following November, the foundations were laid for Australia's second colonial settlement.

It was a bleak time for the local Aboriginal tribespeople, displaced from their lands, but the fertile soil – worked by convicts and managed by pioneering farmers and landowners, such as John and Elizabeth Macarthur – was worth its weight in gold.

By the early 1800s, Parramatta was a bustling landscape of farms, commercial enterprises and government buildings. Macarthur's Elizabeth Farm, built in 1793, Old Government House (1799), and Experiment Farm Cottage (1834) are among a host of historic sites which remain today.

While it never became a centre of government, Parramatta's fortunes rarely waned.

Proclaimed a city in 1936, it remains a vibrant commercial centre, home to 140,000 people, and a major hub for the western suburbs.

The best way to visit Parramatta is by RiverCat from Circular Quay, following the same route as Governor Phillip along the Parramatta River, albeit with a very different landscape.

The pleasant hour-long journey winds past several riverside suburbs, as well as the Olympic Games site at Homebush Bay (see previous page) before the river narrows to a weir, lined on one side by mangroves, at Charles Street Wharf.

Call first at the Parramatta Visitors Centre (see Directions) and pick up a walking map with information on all the historic sites. Allow plenty of time, and wear comfortable walking shoes because the major attractions in Alice Street (Elizabeth Farm), Church Street Mall, George Street, Macquarie Street and Parramatta Regional Park (Old Government House) are spread over a wide area.

Directions Parramatta can be reached by RiverCat from Wharf 5 at Circular Quay. There are regular daily services; the journey takes about an hour (131 500). It's then a five-minute walk from Charles Street Wharf to Parramatta's central business district. Parramatta Visitors Centre is at 346 Church Street (9630 3703), 15 minutes' walk from Charles Street Wharf, open 10am-5pm weekdays, 10am-4pm weekends, stocked with walking maps and historic sites information.

magicmoment

The pleasant RiverCat journey from Circular Quay, following the same route as Governor Arthur Phillip in 1788 along the Parramatta River, albeit with a very different landscape.

mustsee

Old Government House in Parramatta Regional Park (9635 8149), Australia's oldest public building, open weekdays, 10am-4pm, weekends 11am-4pm, $6 adult.

mustdo

Visit Elizabeth Farm, Australia's oldest house, once home to wool pioneers John and Elizabeth Macarthur; 70 Alice Street (9635 9488), open daily, 10am-5pm, $6 adult.

City centre

South Sydney

Many people begin and end their visit in Sydney's south, flying in and out of Sydney Airport, yet few will take the time to explore the area during their stay.

From the air, south Sydney may look like the embodiment of the Great Australian Dream – a seemingly endless suburban sprawl of red-roofed homes, neat gardens and swimming pools on classic quarter-acre blocks – but there's a lot more to the place than meets the eye.

South Sydney boasts two of the city's most beautiful waterways (the Georges River, which flows into Botany Bay, and Port Hacking, which leads to the ocean) and a lifestyle that's hard to beat.

It also holds a special place in the history of modern Australia as the landing place of Captain James Cook in 1770 on the southern headland of Botany Bay. It's one of our Magic Moments and a must-see for anyone with even a passing interest in the nation's colonial history.

For many thousands of years before the arrival of the white settlers, the land around Port Hacking was home to Aborigines and traces of their existence can still be found today. The delightful beachside community of Bundeena, on the southern shores of Port Hacking, leads to the wild and rugged Jibbon Head, where you can find a small but interesting remnant of Aboriginal rock art.

The jewel of south Sydney is the Royal National Park, a glorious expanse of bushland, bushwalking trails, waterfalls, swimming holes and beaches, home to an array of native plants, animals and birdlife. Exploring south Sydney requires a little more time but the rewards are well worth the effort.

At a Glance

For **Captain Cook's Landing Place**, drive out of the city on the Princes Highway, then via Rocky Point Road, Taren Point Road and Captain Cook Drive. It will take about 45 minutes.

Alternatively take the train from Central to Cronulla (the journey lasts about an hour), then board bus 987 outside the train station. Park maps are available from The Discovery Centre (9668 9111) in Botany Bay National Park. A taxi ride from the city costs about $45 one-way.

La Perouse and Bare Island are on the northern headland of Botany Bay. Drive from the city along Anzac Parade and Bunnerong Road or by bus 393 or 394 from Circular Quay. A taxi ride from the city costs about $25 one-way.

For **Bundeena,** board the train from Central to Cronulla and walk along Tonkin Street, next to the train station, to the marina. Cronulla National Park Ferries (9523 2990) operates regular daily return services to Bundeena from 5.30am to 7pm. Pick up the Jibbon Aboriginal Rock Engravings Walk map and leaflet from the cafe near Bundeena Wharf. A taxi ride to Cronulla from the city costs about $40 one-way.

The Royal National Park is 36km south of Sydney and best reached by car. Leave the city on the Princes Highway, then 2.3km south of Sutherland, turn left into the Audley entrance to the park. Entry is $9 a vehicle a day. The Visitor Centre (9542 0648) is open daily, 8.30am-4.30pm.

For bus, train and ferry information: call (131 500). Taxi fares are metered and depend on the level of traffic. These are approximate fares only.

South Sydney's dramatic coastline.

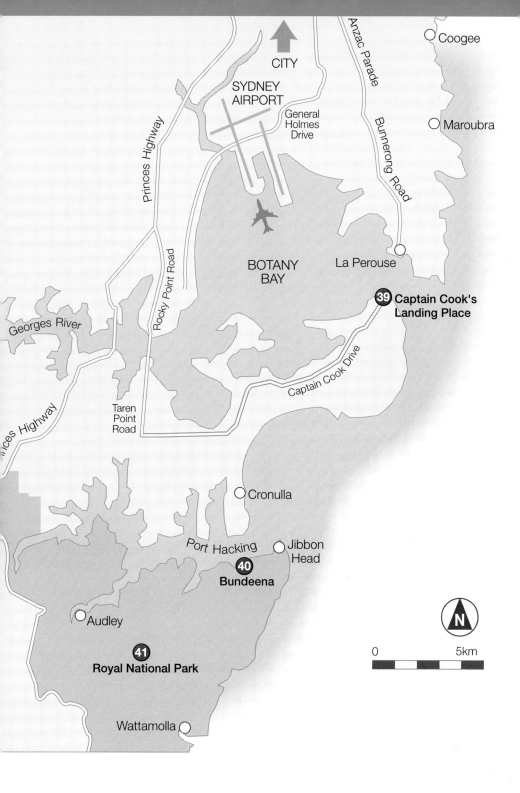

Captain Cook's landing place.

Botany Bay

A little over 200 years separates the modern Botany Bay from the place where Captain James Cook first stepped foot on Australian soil but it might as well be a millennium.

Once blanketed by bushland and occupied by the Aboriginal Dharawal tribe, the horizon is now dominated by a Caltex oil refinery, a strip of hotels and restaurants, and the runways of Sydney International Airport stretching into the bay.

Neither Cook nor his crew of HM Endeavour would recognise the place but their contribution to the foundation of modern Australia is writ large in Botany Bay.

The place where he first stepped ashore at Kurnell on April 29, 1770, on the southern headland of Botany Bay, has been preserved as a monument and holds a special place in the history of modern Australia.

Cook was impressed by what he found in the bay. During an eight-day exploration, the Endeavour's botanists, Sir Joseph Banks and Dr Daniel Solander, recorded many Australian plants and animals for the first time. The botanical find was so great, the place was named Botany Bay.

It was not, however, the site of Australia's first colonial settlement. Eighteen years later, after finding Botany Bay lacked fresh water, the First Fleet sailed north to Sydney Cove in Port Jackson (now Sydney Harbour) and founded the British colony.

Botany Bay's place in history was not forgotten. In 1899, 100 hectares of land at Kurnell was set aside as a public nature reserve and monuments erected to Cook, his crew and the Aborigines who lived in the area.

The Discovery Centre, in the centre of Captain Cook's Landing Place, is your best starting point with exhibitions and visitor information. A series of easy marked walks lead from the centre.

The Banks-Solander Track, a 500m boardwalk, follows in the footsteps of the renowned botanists to reveal an abundance of native plants and wildflowers including the banksia, named after Sir Joseph Banks.

The 2km Monument Track offers a pleasant walk along the tree-lined foreshores of Botany Bay.

A stone tablet marks where Cook stepped ashore in 1770 and a buoy shows where the Endeavour dropped anchor.

La Perouse, on the northern headland of Botany Bay, also has great historical and Aboriginal cultural signifiance.

There's a museum commemorating the ill-fated expedition of French explorer La Perouse in 1788 and the historic battlements on nearby Bare Island, said to be haunted, are also worth visiting (9311 3379).

Directions For Captain Cook's Landing Place, drive out of the city on the Princes Highway, then via Rocky Point Road, Taren Point Road and Captain Cook Drive. Alternatively take the train from Central to Cronulla (131 500), then bus 987 from outside the train station. Park maps are available from The Discovery Centre (9668 9111), close to the Landing Place. For La Perouse and Bare Island, drive from the city along Anzac Parade and Bunnerong Road or by bus 393 or 394 from Circular Quay.

magicmoment

Sitting on the rocks where Captain James Cook first stepped ashore in Australia in 1770.

mustsee

The native wildflowers and plants along the Banks-Solander boardwalk, first recorded by botanists Sir Joseph Banks and Dr Daniel Solander in 1770.

mustdo

The Cape Baily Walking Track, a 5km walk alongside heathland, sand dunes, deep gorges, Aboriginal "middens" and sandstone cliffs.

Bundeena

magicmoment

Enjoying a picnic on Jibbon Head and watching the surf of the Pacific Ocean crashing against the rock ledge and cliffs.

mustsee

The Jibbon Aboriginal rock engravings, carved by the Dharawal people and thought to be up to 5,000 years old.

mustdo

Swim at Jibbon Beach, a delightful crescent of sand and calm water, far from the madding crowds of the city beaches.

This terrific day-trip combines beach and bush, a delightful ferry ride, ancient Aboriginal rock engravings and it can all be done by public transport. The gateway to Bundeena is Cronulla, the most southerly of Sydney's major suburbs, a bustling centre with a breezy beachside atmosphere.

Bundeena, a tiny community nestled next to the thick bushland of the Royal National Park, is reached by a 30-minute ferry ride from Cronulla's Tonkin Street Wharf. Cronulla National Park Ferries (see Directions) operates a fleet of wooden ferries which chug across Gunnamatta Bay and Port Hacking.

The ferry ride is a delight in itself, passing alongside imposing homes and tropical gardens before heading into the open waters of Port Hacking, but it's the Jibbon Walk from Bundeena Wharf which is the highlight.

The trail, marked on a free National Parks leaflet available from the cafe near the wharf, winds along The Avenue and Lambeth Walk to Jibbon Beach, a wonderful stretch of bush-fringed sand and calm water which is ideal for swimming.

The trail continues at the eastern end of the beach to Jibbon Head, offering magnificent coastal views the further you walk. You'll brush by thick vegetation, vast spiders webs (the spiders are harmless but best left undisturbed) and small snakes and lizards may appear but this is classic Australian coastal bush at its best.

The trail runs in a loop to a collection of Aboriginal rock engravings carved onto an open rock ledge. The outlines are faint but clear enough to reveal the shapes of whales, stingrays, a kangaroo and a six-fingered male figure thought to be an Aboriginal mythical spirit.

Before white settlement, the region was inhabited by the Dharawal people, controlled by a complex set of rituals under the influence of Daramulan, the "All Father".

This engraving site is one of about 80 around Port Hacking. Charcoal found in a rock shelter near Jibbon Head has been dated at 8,000 years old. While the engravings are thought to be up to 5,000 years old, it's possible the Dharawal people lived here for 30,000 years.

The trail leads from the engravings to Jibbon Head, a rugged cliff offering expansive views of the Pacific Ocean (see Magic Moment). Return via the trail to the beach and wharf.

Take swimming gear, a hat and sunscreen; there's food and drink at the Bundeena Wharf cafe. On your return to Cronulla, you can dine in a choice of restaurants and cafes. You'll find a pleasant beach, park, two rock pools, a coastal walk and accommodation if you want to stay longer.

Directions Board the train from Central to Cronulla; the journey takes about an hour (131 500). Walk along Tonkin Street, next to the train station, to the marina. Cronulla National Park Ferries (9523 2990) operates regular daily return services to Bundeena from 5.30am-7pm, about 30 minutes each way. Pick up the Jibbon Aboriginal Rock Engravings Walk map and leaflet from the cafe near Bundeena Wharf.

Gunyah Beach, next to Bundeena Wharf.

The beautiful Wattamolla Falls

Royal National Park

This is one of the jewels in Sydney's crown yet few visitors take the time to discover it.

Those who do are rewarded handsomely with beautiful coastal bushland, surf beaches, freshwater swimming holes, walking trails and more than 700 species of plants and 200 species of birds.

Established in 1879, on the south coast of Sydney, the park has the distinction of being the first national park in Australia and the second in the world, after Yellowstone in the United States.

While Yellowstone was established in 1872, it was not officially designated as a national park until 1883, four years after its Australian counterpart, which means the Royal can by rights claim to be the world's first national park. The Royal title was bestowed by Queen Elizabeth during her visit to Australia in 1954.

The park's history extends far beyond white settlement, occupied for hundreds of generations by the Aboriginal Dharawal tribe who used the sandstone caves for shelter and fished the coast, estuaries and streams. The bush supplemented this diet with vegetable and animal foods.

By the 1870s, 100 years after European settlement, the city of Sydney had grown at such an alarming rate the then NSW Premier, Sir John Robertson, realised the need for a people's park, a green space where people could escape the crowds, vermin and disease of the city.

The park today is a wild landscape of cliffs, creeks, beaches, streams, plateaus and deep river valleys, comprising more than 16,000 hectares of coastal heath vegetation, woodland and sedgeland, open forests, rainforests and mangroves.

The park is criss-crossed with walking trails leading to the Hacking River, along the coast or deep into the bush, brimming with native plants and wildlife.

It's is also an excellent place for bird-watching. If you sit quietly with a pair of binoculars, you may catch a glimpse of lyrebirds, green catbirds, satin bowerbirds, golden whistlers, top-knot pigeons, brown cuckoo-doves, and yellow-throated scrub-wren.

While walking, it's worth remembering the park was ravaged by severe bushfires in 1994. Its remarkable recovery is testament to the power of nature in a land where fire plays such a vital role in the regeneration process.

Surf, swim, fish, cycle and bushwalk, hire row boats and canoes, or simply take a picnic and relax at a tranquil water hole. Carry good walking shoes, a hat, sunscreen and plenty of water if you're doing a longer walk. Check at the visitor centre at Audley for park maps.

Directions The Royal National Park is 36km south of Sydney and best reached by car. Leave the city on the Princes Highway; 2.3km south of Sutherland, turn left into the Audley entrance to the park. Entry is $9 a vehicle a day. The Visitor Centre (9542 0648) is your best starting point with rangers on hand to offer advice and information on walking trails, wildlife and birdlife, beaches and freshwater swimming pools. The visitor centre is open daily, 8.30am-4.30pm.

magicmoment

Swimming at one of the great beaches, especially Wattamolla Cove and Bonnie Vale, or the freshwater Blue, Karloo, Deer, Curracurrang or Crystal pools.

mustsee

Surfers riding the waves at Garie Beach. Beware dangerous currents; the beach is patrolled only on weekends and public holidays during summer.

mustdo

Lady Carrington Drive, a 9.6km walk which winds alongside the Hacking River through rainforest and woodlands.

Blue Mountains

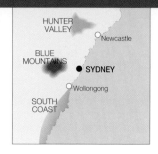

N o visit to Sydney would be complete without a trip to the Blue Mountains, an ancient wilderness with sandstone cliffs, tree-shrouded valleys, waterfalls, walking trails, quaint villages, dramatic views and the iconic Three Sisters rock formations.

Located about 100 kilometres or a 90-minute drive west of Sydney, the mountains are an unspoilt landscape of deep valleys and rugged escarpments, tinged blue by eucalytus oil rising off the canopy of trees and refracting the sun's rays.

Rising more than 1,000 metres above sea level, the Blue Mountains are steeped in Aboriginal legend and pioneering history. Tales of hardy explorers, such as Lawson, Blaxland and Wentworth, who carved a path through the dense bushland in 1813 to open up the fertile lands of the western plains, are the stuff of local folklore.

The region's cool climate made it an ideal summer retreat for Sydneysiders keen to escape the heat of the coast and, with the arrival of the railway in the 1860s, a scattering of villages, complete with cottages and flower-filled gardens, were established.

It's that heritage which remains today in a collection of bustling communities, such as Katoomba, Blackheath, Leura and Mount Wilson, offering bed-and-breakfast accommodation, arts and crafts galleries, cafes and restaurants, and backed by the untamed wilderness of the Blue Mountains National Park.

The mountains are a place for the seasons, sometimes all four in one day, brimming with cherry blossom in spring, lush greenery in summer, ablaze with autumn foliage and shrouded in winter mists and occasional snow.

Above all, it's a place to relax, breathe in the fresh mountain air and enjoy the beautiful scenery.

Charming accommodation.

At a Glance

The easiest way to reach the **Blue Mountains** from Sydney is by car, via the M4 Motorway and Great Western Highway. There are daily train services (131 500) but it's hard to explore the mountains without a car. Several coach companies and 4WD adventure operators offer day trips from Sydney.

You can return to Sydney via the northerly **Bells Line of Road** if you want to take in the historic Zig Zag Railway steam train at Clarence, the charming village of Mount Wilson, and beautiful Mount Tomah Botanic Gardens.

There are scores of accommodation options in the Blue Mountains. Standards and service vary dramatically from the five-star Lilianfels at Echo Point, Katoomba (see page 124), to no-star B&Bs. There are **Blue Mountains Visitor Information Centres** on the Great Western Highway at Glenbrook, open daily 8.30am-5pm, Sunday 4.30pm, and on Echo Point Road, Katoomba, open daily 9am-5pm (1300 653 408).

The **Blue Mountains National Park** covers 218,100 hectares of wilderness. If you want to go bushwalking, check first at the **National Parks and Wildlife Service Heritage Centre,** Govetts Leap Road, Blackheath, (02) 4787 8877, open daily, 9am-4.30pm, for maps and advice. Remember to take a hat, sunscreen, good walking shoes and water.

Yulefest, a delightful Christmas celebration in the middle of the year, runs during the winter months of June to August.

The mountains are prone to heavy **mists** at various times of year which can obliterate the spectacular views. Check weather conditions in advance of your visit.

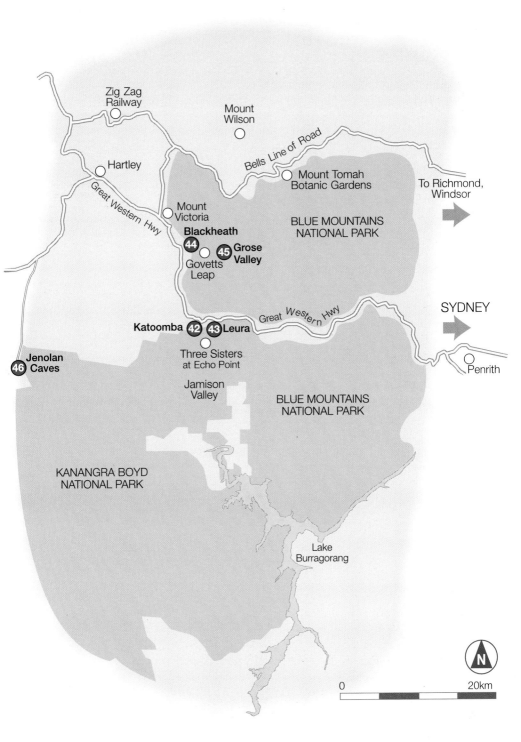

The majestic Three Sisters at Echo Point.

Katoomba

There are three good reasons to start your Blue Mountains exploration in Katoomba and they all come etched in sandstone. The majestic Three Sisters at Echo Point, a unique rock formation consisting of a trio of pinnacles towering over the Jamison Valley, are widely considered the highlight of the mountains.

The view from Echo Point Lookout, stretching across the southern half of the Blue Mountains National Park, is simply breathtaking. Day or night, when the pinnacles are bathed in an ethereal orange light, the Three Sisters are a sight to behold.

The bustling town of Katoomba lies in the heart of the Blue Mountains, sitting atop the main plateau which separates the Grose Valley in the northern section of the national park and the Jamison Valley to the south.

The town centre is set around Katoomba Street, leading from the railway station, a reminder of the glory days when Sydneysiders would flock by train to the popular holiday resort town to escape the heat of the summer. Katoomba's star has waned, however, largely because many people visit the mountains only for a day, and the once grand buildings, Art Deco facades and cafes have a faded elegance about them.

The Three Sisters lie just to the south of Katoomba, off Echo Point Road, best seen in the early morning or late afternoon when the tourist crowds aren't jostling for elbow room.

There are several walks from here – the Prince Henry Cliff Walk to the Scenic Skyway and Railway; the Giant Stairway down 980 steps to the valley; the Federal Pass and Dardanelles Pass – but most people simply take in the wonderful Echo Point view. Check at the information centre for walking maps and advice.

The Scenic Skyway and Railway, in Violet Street, are popular attractions offering rides on a cable car over the Jamison Valley and Katoomba Falls and on the world's steepest incline train track, and there are many wonderful lookouts throughout the area. Cliff Drive winds along the edge of the Jamison Valley offering more panoramas from the comfort of your car.

Leave time to browse in Katoomba – the marvellously kitsch Paragon Cafe (56 Katoomba Street) and Avalon Restaurant (98 Main Street) are fun – and there are some good antique galleries.

The Edge Maxvision cinema (Great Western Highway) features a film of the mountains on a six storey screen but nothing beats standing on the edge of the Jamison Valley and seeing it for yourself.

Directions The best way to reach Katoomba from Sydney is by car, via the M4 Motorway and Great Western Highway. There are train services (131 500) but it's hard to explore beyond Katoomba without a car. Several coach companies and 4WD adventure operators offer day trips from Sydney. There are Blue Mountains Visitor Information Centres on the Great Western Highway at Glenbrook, open daily 8.30am-5pm, Sunday 4.30pm, and on Echo Point Road, Katoomba, open daily 9am-5pm (1300 653 408).

magicmoment
Watching the mountain mists rise up from the valley and swirl around the Three Sisters at Echo Point. Check out the Aboriginal legend surrounding the marvellous rock formation at the visitor centre.

mustsee
The views of the Jamison Valley and Katoomba Falls from the Scenic Skyway and Railway, $4.50 adult, (02) 4782 2699.

mustdo
The Giant Stairway from Echo Point down into the Jamison Valley. Be warned: there are 980 steps one-way.

Leura

43

magicmoment

The view from Sublime Point, overlooking the majestic Jamison Valley.

mustsee

The tree-lined Leura Mall, especially in spring or autumn, with its charming restaurants, cafes, galleries and craft shops.

mustdo

A visit to Everglades Gardens, 37 Everglades Ave, open daily, 10am-4pm (spring and summer 5pm), $5 adult, (02) 4784 1938.

Arguably the prettiest village in the Blue Mountains, Leura has long been a magnet for artists and writers who are drawn by the peaceful surroundings and inspired by the natural beauty of the mountain landscapes.

A few kilometres east of Katoomba, Leura is also a drawcard for tourists and day-trippers who come to browse in its charming art and craft galleries, bookshops and antique stores, dine in its cosy restaurants and cafes and explore some of the best gardens in the Blue Mountains.

Leura is especially pretty in spring or autumn, when the main Leura Mall is a riot of cherry blossom or autumn foliage, and many of the private and public gardens are looking their best. You could spend a very pleasant morning or afternoon strolling along the mall and browsing in its shops. A drive around Leura's residential streets, many lined with beautiful weatherboard homes and cottage gardens, is a must.

Just south of Leura Mall lies Leuralla (36 Olympian Parade), an Art Deco mansion boasting one of Australia's finest collections of toys and dolls. The historic house is also a railway museum and has a pleasant landscaped garden.

Leura is also home to the wonderful Everglades Gardens (see Must Do), established in the 1930s by the Danish landscape designer Paul Sorensen. The five-hectare estate includes an imposing house and gardens, grotto pool, picnic grounds, lookouts and views of the Jamison Valley. The gardens have a gallery, gift shop, tea rooms and museum.

Leura Markets are held on the first Sunday of each month while Leura Fair and Garden Festival, when many private gardens are open for public inspection, is held every October.

Like Katoomba, Leura borders the Jamison Valley and offers panoramic views over the southern half of the Blue Mountains National Park. From Leuralla, you can drive further along Olympian Parade to Bridal Veil and Gordon Falls lookouts, for more views over the Jamison Valley, or you can head along Cliff Drive to Katoomba and the Three Sisters, stopping at the pretty Leura Cascades along the way.

Alternatively, head from Everglades Gardens along Sublime Point Road to the lookout at Sublime Point. The early pioneers didn't think up these names for nothing. The view from the lookout is, well, sublime.

There is good accommodation in Leura, from the popular Fairmont Resort to cottages and B&Bs, if you want to stay longer; contact the Visitor Information Centre. Silk's Brasserie, 128 The Mall, (02) 4784 2534, is an excellent restaurant.

Directions The best way to reach Leura from Sydney is by car, via the M4 Motorway and Great Western Highway. There are daily train services (131 500) but it's hard to explore beyond Leura without a car. Many coach companies include Leura in their Blue Mountains itineraries. There are Blue Mountains Visitor Information Centres on the Great Western Highway at Glenbrook, open daily 8.30am-5pm, Sunday 4.30pm, and on Echo Point Road, Katoomba, open daily 9am-5pm (1300 653 408).

Browse in the galleries and craft stores in Leura Mall.

Explore rugged bushland.

Blackheath

You might think of driving past this unassuming village, straddling the busy Great Western Highway, but it's the gateway to some of the greatest natural treasures in the Blue Mountains.

Take a right-hand turn off the highway down Evans Lookout Road, Govetts Leap Road or Hat Hill Road in Blackheath and you'll be rewarded with views that will take your breath away.

The Jamison Valley to the south may have the Three Sisters, scenic waterfalls and panoramic views but when it comes to sheer untamed wilderness on a grand and majestic scale, the Grose Valley to the north wins hands down every time. There are so many lookouts, bushwalking trails and photo opportunities, a visit to Blackheath should be at the top of your Blue Mountains must-see list.

The drive to Blackheath, about 10 kilometres north of Katoomba, is not without note. Two kilometres from Katoomba (on the left side of the highway) is the Explorers Marked Tree, a poignant monument commemorating the crossing of the Blue Mountains in 1813 by the legendary explorers Lawson, Blaxland and Wentworth.

A pathway leads from the tree through bushland to a simple graveyard with several unmarked graves, the final resting place for convicts who died working on the building of the road.

Blackheath isn't the prettiest village in the mountains but it doesn't pretend to be either. It's a lively community set around a commercial centre at the highway end of Govetts Leap Road and has some pleasant houses and gardens tucked away in its leafy streets.

The village centre also has a modest antique gallery at the historic Victory Theatre (there's a colourful mural by renowned local artist Jenny Kee down one side of the theatre) and other general stores, cafes and restaurants.

Blackheath is an excellent base for exploring the Grose Valley (see next page) and has some good bed-and-breakfast accommodation and a couple of excellent (if expensive) luxury guest houses: Cleopatra, (02) 4787 8456, a charming historic homestead, and Parklands, (02) 4787 7771, an English-style country estate, are recommended.

Blackheath is also home to Vulcan's, one of the best restaurants in the Blue Mountains (see Must Do). It's open for breakfast, lunch and dinner on Friday, Saturday and Sunday (bookings essential) but we suggest dinner after a bracing bushwalk in the Grose Valley. The restaurant is BYO (bring your own wine).

The National Parks and Wildlife Service Heritage Centre, (02) 4787 8877, is at the valley end of Govetts Leap Road.

Directions The best way to reach Blackheath from Sydney is by car, via the M4 Motorway and Great Western Highway. There are daily train services (131 500) but it's hard to explore beyond Blackheath without a car. Some coach companies include Blackheath in their Blue Mountains itineraries. There are Blue Mountains Visitor Information Centres on the Great Western Highway at Glenbrook, open daily 8.30am-5pm, Sunday 4.30pm, and on Echo Point Road, Katoomba, open daily 9am-5pm (1300 653 408).

magicmoment

The short walk along the edge of the Grose Valley from Govetts Leap Lookout to the wispy Bridal Veil Falls.

mustsee

The Explorers Marked Tree, on the Great Western Highway between Katoomba and Blackheath, commemorating the crossing of the Blue Mountains by Lawson, Blaxland and Wentworth in 1813.

mustdo

Dinner at Vulcan's Restaurant, 33 Govetts Leap Road, open Friday, Saturday and Sunday, (02) 4787 6899.

Grose Valley

magicmoment

Standing on the
lookout at
Pulpit Rock with
its sweeping 280
degree views of
the Grose Valley.

mustsee

Perrys Lookout
and Anvil Rock
at the end of
Hat Hill Road.

mustdo

The clifftop
Pulpit Rock Track,
about three
hours return, or
the Grand Canyon
Walk deep into
the valley, about
three to four
hours.

There are many wonderful natural attractions scattered across the Blue Mountains but the Grose Valley is in a league of its own. The majestic panoramas of towering sandstone cliffs, delicate waterfalls and a carpet of thick bushland sliced by the Grose River are simply stunning.

The Australian bush is at its best here, brimming with tiny wildflowers, fragrant eucalyptus trees, flocks of native birds and elusive marsupials. It's a place where nature rules supreme, a *Jurassic Park*-type landscape which has remained largely undisturbed for millions of years.

The beauty of the Grose Valley is twofold. You can enjoy its sweeping views simply by stepping out of your car and strolling over to one of the many lookouts along the clifftop or you can slip on the walking shoes and head off for a bracing bushwalk.

If you decide to go walking, the rewards are untold. Several tracks run from the three main lookouts at the end of Evans Lookout Road, Govetts Leap Road and Hat Hill Road, Blackheath, offering a variety of graded and marked trails.

Some walks, like the three-hour Pulpit Rock Track, wind from Govetts Leap Lookout around the clifftop. Others like the majestic Grand Canyon, a four-hour hike from Neates Glen to Evans Lookout (or vice versa), descend onto the valley floor.

Whichever trail you take depends on your level of fitness and stamina but there's something for everyone. One of the prettiest and easiest walks is from Govetts Leap Lookout along the clifftop to the wispy Bridal Veil Falls. You can continue along Cliff Top Track to Evans Lookout or turn right at the falls and head along the delightful woodland and heathland Braeside Walk.

The Grand Canyon is a considerable walk in either direction and involves scores of steps in or out of the valley at the Evans Lookout end. The canyon can be damp and slippery after rain, so caution is advised, but it's a magnificent walk alongside ancient mosses, ferns, rainforest, eucalypt forest, gullies, waterfalls and streams. Native birdlife includes the elusive lyrebird and whipbird.

The Pulpit Rock Track is a favourite because it combines sweeping clifftop views with waterfalls, scribbly gums, delicate wildflowers and intricate weather-beaten rocks. If the conditions are good, the 280-degree view of the Grose Valley from the lookout at Pulpit Rock is marvellous.

Call at the Heritage Centre (see Directions) for walking maps and advice. Be warned, some tracks have steep stairs and steps, loose soil and natural hazards. The weather can also change quickly and dramatically, so wear the appropriate layered clothing.

Directions From Blackheath, drive along Evans Lookout Road, Govetts Leap Road or Hat Hill Road to the lookouts over the valley. Marked and graded trails lead from each lookout. The National Parks and Wildlife Service Heritage Centre, (02) 4787 8877, is at the valley end of Govetts Leap Road, open daily, 9am-4.30pm. Remember to carry a hat, sunscreen, good walking shoes and water.

Marvel at the views or head off on a bracing bushwalk.

GRAND CANYON
WALKING TRACK →

EVANS LOOKOUT
3 HOURS →

GRAND CANYON
GROSE VALLEY →

One of the many extraordinary formations in Jenolan Caves.

Jenolan Caves

Adjacent to Kanangra Boyd National Park, just to the west of the Blue Mountains National Park, lie Jenolan Caves, a network of more than 300 limestone caves, nine of which have been progressively opened to the public over the past 150 years.

Believed to have been first explored by European settlers in 1838, the caves are one of the most popular attractions in the Blue Mountains. A total of nine show caves, brimming with bizarre limestone formations, are open for tours and should be high on a must-see list of a visit to the area.

The widest and highest known chambers in the system are in the Lucas Cave, regarded as the best general cave because of the variety of formations and chambers, including The Cathedral, Slide, Broken Column, Proscenium and River Styx, which offer a good representation of all of Jenolan's main features and part of its river system.

Which caves you choose to see depends on your fitness and stamina. The Imperial Cave is the least strenuous, a long and ancient dry river passage with smooth tunnel-like sections and many attractive cave scenes. It's ideal for the elderly and disabled because of its gentle gradients.

The Chifley Cave, illuminated by electric light in 1880, is mildly strenuous along with the Orient Cave and Temple of Baal. The most strenuous caves are the River Cave and Jubilee Cave but these have some unique and extraordinary formations.

All provide a glimpse of nature running riot with biblical and mythological names like Lot's Wife, Bath of Venus, The Shrine, Gabriel's Wing, Pool of Reflections and Moloch's Grotto adding to the mystery and intrigue of the cave system.

Our favourite is the Temple of Baal (see Magic Moment), discovered in 1904 and containing The Angel's Wing, Jenolan's largest known shawl formation. The cave is an enormous dome cavern with some of the most delicate features in the entire cave system.

Most visitors will do a guided tour, lasting between one and two hours, but if you want to explore deeper into the underground system there are challenging adventure tours.

For these tours, you'll need to be reasonably fit and bring suitable clothing, such as overalls and good footwear, but other equipment will be provided. There are also historical tours which are very atmospheric.

If you want to stay longer, the imposing Jenolan Caves House offers accommodation close to the caves entrance and there are motel, cabin and cottage options nearby.

Jenolan Caves are surrounded by a 2,416-hectare wildlife reserve which has some excellent bushwalks. The historic village of Hartley, close to the turn-off for the twisty Jenolan Caves Road, is also worth exploring.

Directions Jenolan Caves are a two-and-a-half drive west of Sydney, via the Great Western Highway or Bells Line of Road, and Jenolan Caves Road, near Hartley. There are coach tours from Sydney and Katoomba. Cave tours start from $12 adult; contact the Guides Office, (02) 6359 3311.

46

magicmoment

Entering the Temple of Baal, an enormous dome cavern with five impressive cave features, including the legendary Angel's Wing, Jenolan's largest known shawl formation.

mustsee

The Lucas Cave with the widest and highest known chambers in the system boasting most of the main types of formations.

mustdo

An adventure tour using ropes, ladders and abseiling to explore the underground caves in much the same way the early explorers found them. Not for the faint-hearted.

Hunter Valley

Picture the scene. You're in the middle of a winery with rows of vines stretching away into the distance. The picnic rug is laid out on the ground. You've got bread, meats, cheese and fruit, a chilled bottle of semillon, and the sun is shining down from a cloudless sky. It feels like God's Own Country and indeed it is.

Welcome to the Hunter Valley, one of Australia's prime wine-producing areas and the perfect day or weekend escape from the madding crowds of Sydney. Nestled in rolling countryside, an easy two-hour drive to the north-west of the city, the Hunter Valley is a peaceful haven of lush vineyards, bush-covered ranges and excellent guest houses and restaurants.

Named after a former NSW Governor, John Hunter, the region was a major coal-producing centre but the decline of coal has left the industry a shadow of its former self.

The wine business, started from a few hundred European vine cuttings in the 1830s, has proved to be an ongoing success story with Hunter vintages, especially the signature semillon variety, winning local and international prizes and gracing dining tables around the world.

It may not produce Australia's best wine – that accolade arguably belongs to South Australia's Barossa Valley – but it's a fine drop complemented by beautiful scenery, more than 70 wineries, great food, activities from horse-riding to hot-air ballooning and those all-important wine-tastings.

You could spend a few days exploring the nearby Barrington Tops National Park, the historic city of Newcastle, and the beaches and bays of Port Stephens, but if you like your wine, the Hunter Valley makes for the perfect grape escape.

At a Glance

The quickest and easiest way to reach the **Hunter Valley** from Sydney is by car, a two-hour drive via the Pacific Highway and Newcastle Freeway, following signs for Cessnock. You can also turn off the Freeway at Peats Ridge and take the country route via Wollombi to Cessnock. There are daily train services to Newcastle, Maitland, Cessnock and Scone (131 500) but it's hard to explore the Hunter Valley without a car.

You can visit the Hunter Valley in a day-trip but we recommend staying at least one night in the area, especially if you are wine-tasting. Several coach companies offer day tours from Sydney.

There are lots of **accommodation** options in the Hunter Valley, ranging from resort-style hotels to cosy B&Bs. We recommend the Hunter Resort (see page 124) in Hermitage Road, Pokolbin, nestled in its own vineyard. **Cessnock Visitor Information Centre,** Aberdare Road, (02) 4990 4477, can advise on options, open weekdays 9am to 5pm, Saturday 9.30am to 5pm, Sunday 9.30am to 3.30pm; www.winecountry.com.au

Many wineries offer wine-tastings and cellar-door sales, and some offer winery tours. There's also a range of **activities** from cycling to bushwalking and 4WD adventure tours.

The **Hunter Valley Harvest Festival,** an annual celebration of the wine industry, is held in March and April. It's a fun time to be in the area but also very busy.

Barrington Tops National Park is a 90 minute drive north of the Hunter Valley; **Newcastle** about 45 minutes south-east; **Port Stephens** about 75 minutes east.

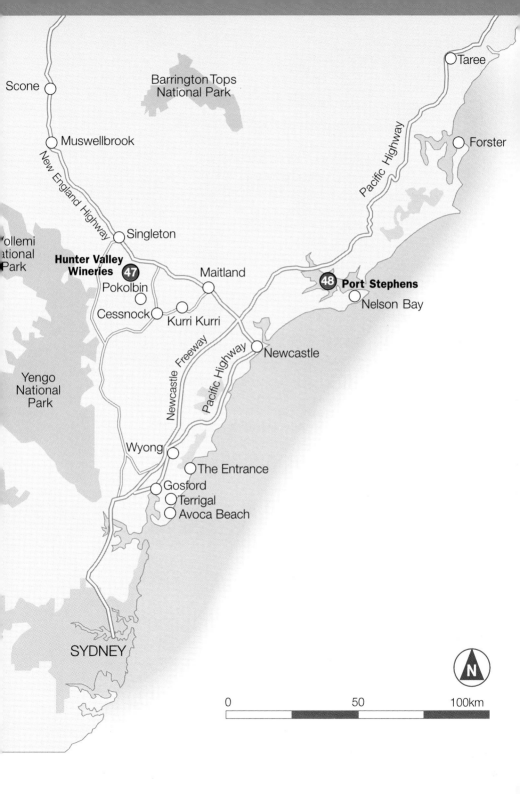

The rolling vines of the Hunter Valley.

The Wineries

If you're looking for a vintage escape, you can't go past the Hunter Valley. Nestled in the shadow of the Great Dividing Range, about two hours' drive north-west of Sydney, the Hunter offers the chance to sample some of Australia's best wines amid a truly beautiful rural setting.

Framed by the bush-covered Brokenback Ranges, the Hunter Valley is a picture-postcard landscape of rolling vineyards, historic wineries, quaint villages, cosy bed-and-breakfast accommodation, fine restaurants and a thoroughly relaxed and peaceful atmosphere.

The sense of tranquillity belies the daily hive of activity in the vineyards for this is the oldest and one of the most productive wine regions in Australia. Wine-making is a multi-million-dollar industry in the Hunter Valley and the lifeblood of many people who live here. For the visitor, it offers the chance to sample some excellent table wines, dine on fresh local produce, explore the pretty countryside and enjoy a range of activities, as well as taking time out to relax and breathe in the fresh country air.

The area is split into two distinct regions, the Upper and Lower Hunter Valley, with farmlands and renowned horse studs to the north and the winelands to the south. The gateway to the wineries is Cessnock with most of the vineyards scattered around the neighbouring Pokolbin. First stop should be the Cessnock Tourist Information Centre (see Directions) which can provide all the information you'll need about the wineries and surrounding Hunter Valley. It's a distinctive yellow building in Aberdare Road.

Armed with a wineries map, you can then tour at leisure, stopping at any vineyard which takes your fancy. Many offer wine-tastings and cellar-door sales and some offer guided tours. You don't have to book, just turn up on the day.

Most of the colonial vineyards, first planted in the 1830s, have disappeared but many historic wineries are still going strong. The names of the 70-odd wine producers, including Lindemans, Tyrrells, Tullochs, McGuigan, Rothbury, Oakdale, McWilliams and Draytons, roll off the tongue like a fruity Hunter semillon.

There are many excellent hotels and restaurants – Casuarina, (02) 4998 7888; Pepper Tree and The Convent (see Must See); Peppers Guest House, (02) 4998 7596; and The Hunter Resort (see page 124) are among the best.

If you really want to see the Hunter Valley in full swing, the annual Hunter Harvest Festival is held in March and April but it's a hectic time for the winemakers, so don't expect their undivided attention.

Directions It's a two-hour drive from Sydney to the Hunter Valley, via the Pacific Highway and Newcastle Freeway, then follow signs for Cessnock. There are train services to Newcastle, Maitland, Cessnock and Scone (131 500) but it's hard to explore the Hunter Valley without a car. Coach and 4WD companies offer day tours from Sydney. Cessnock Tourist Information Centre, Aberdare Road, can advise on accommodation and activities, (02) 4990 4477, open weekdays 9am-5pm, Saturday 9.30am-5pm, Sunday 9.30am-3.30pm.

magicmoment

Flying over the Hunter Valley in a hot-air balloon at sunrise, followed by a celebration champagne breakfast. Balloon Aloft, toll-free (1800 028 568), from $200 a person, advance bookings essential.

mustsee

Pepper Tree, Halls Road, Pokolbin, (02) 4998 7539, a pretty boutique winery with an 1870s cottage, restaurant and gardens.

The Convent, a five-star hotel, (02) 4998 7764, once a Brigidine convent, is close by.

mustdo

A leisurely horse-and-carriage or bicycle tour of the vineyards. Contact the Cessnock Tourist Information Centre, (02) 4990 4477, for details.

Port Stephens

magicmoment

Seeing bottlenose
dolphins splashing
in the waters
of Port Stephens;
dolphin-watch
cruises depart
D'Albora Marina,
bookings through
the visitor centre
(see Directions).

mustsee

The panoramic
views of Nelson
Bay and Port
Stephens from
Gan Gan Lookout.

mustdo

A swim at the
impossibly blue
Salamander,
Shoal, Fingal
or Anna bays,
especially in
summer.

If you want to see more than the wineries of the Hunter Valley, it makes sense to stay longer and explore the lovely coastal peninsula of Port Stephens and Nelson Bay, to the north of Newcastle.

An easy 75-minute drive north-east of the wineries, Port Stephens is one of the most scenic bays in Australia. Almost five times the size of Sydney Harbour, Port Stephens is a stretch of impossibly blue water edged by chalk-white sands and bush-covered headlands.

The combination of calm water, unspoilt beaches, relaxed bayside communities, surf beaches, good bushwalking country, diverse tours and attractions and the lure of the wineries close by, has made Port Stephens a summer holiday mecca for Sydney families.

Summer or winter, Port Stephens is very beautiful. On a cloudless day, when the sun shimmers on the surface of the water, the bay is the sort of classic panorama which makes Australia the envy of the world.

You could chill out on the powdery sands of Salamander and Shoal Bay on the harbour side of the peninsula or hit the surf of Fingal and Anna bays on the ocean side and revel in a couple of days by the beach but you'd be missing out on a host of activities.

One of the best tours is a cruise to watch dolphins from the main marina at Nelson Bay (see Magic Moment). The crystal-clear waters of Port Stephens are home to a community of bottlenose dolphins which swim to the surface and frolic around passing yachts and charter boats.

A number of operators offer dolphin-watch cruises year-round; you can book through the Port Stephens Visitor Centre (see Directions) which has a board displaying all the tours on offer each day. The dolphin cruises are especially good if you're travelling with children.

During the winter months, several operators offer terrific whale-watching cruises to view the migrating humpback and southern right whales as they pass Port Stephens on their way to calving grounds in Queensland's Hervey Bay.

Away from the water, there's bushwalking in Tomaree National Park on the northern tip of the peninsula and for magnificent 360 degree views of Port Stephens and coastline head up to Gan Gan Lookout, just outside Nelson Bay.

There's a variety of accommodation in the area from five-star resort hotels like The Anchorage at Corlette, (02) 4984 2555, a Cape Cod-style complex with its own marina and boardwalks, to motels and holiday rental apartments. There's also Bardots Nude Village Resort, (02) 4982 2000, if you're so inclined but this is probably best visited in summer...

Directions The best way to reach Port Stephens from Sydney is via the Pacific Highway and Newcastle Freeway and follow signs for Raymond Terrace or Nelson Bay, just after Newcastle. There are trains and buses from Sydney (131 500) but it's hard to explore Port Stephens without a car. Port Stephens Visitors Centre, Victoria Parade, Nelson Bay, (02) 4981 1579, can advise on accommodation, tours and attractions.

The Anchorage.

Summer fun.

Spot the dolphin.

South Coast

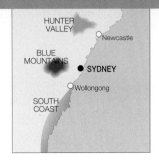

We don't like to shout too loudly about the NSW South Coast because we'd really like to keep the place to ourselves. While visitors flock to the natural grandeur of the Blue Mountains and wineries of the Hunter Valley, the beautiful Southern Highlands and South Coast are often overlooked.

A popular weekend escape for Sydneysiders, this delightful region is brimming with so many wonderful attractions it's hard to know where to begin.

Take the Hume Highway from Sydney through the Southern Highlands and you can wallow in a landscape of pretty villages, rolling hills, mist-shrouded valleys, vast tracts of rugged wilderness and farmlands dotted with cattle.

The main towns and villages – Bowral, Berrima, Mittagong, Moss Vale, Bundanoon, Burrawang, Braemar and Robertson – are awash with historic buildings, cottages and gardens, antique stores, art galleries, cosy guest houses and restaurants serving fresh country produce. Morton National Park, home to the spectacular Fitzroy Falls, boasts some wonderful views and bushwalking trails while the tranquil Kangaroo Valley offers a slice of rural life with a cool-climate twist.

Alternatively, take the Princes Highway along the South Coast and you'll find a picture-postcard collection of beachside communities and fishing villages framed by some of the most beautiful beaches and bushland in Australia.

It's a 90-minute drive from Sydney to Kiama, a three-hour drive to Jervis Bay, and the same again to the southern reaches of Narooma, Merimbula and Eden but the rewards are untold. There are rainforests and waterfalls, bays and lakes, endless stretches of golden (and in some places chalk-white) sand, dolphins, kangaroos, migrating whales and other native wildlife, all wrapped up in a thoroughly relaxed and laidback atmosphere.

Hyams Beach, Jervis Bay.

At a Glance

You can combine a visit to the Southern Highlands and South Coast but you'll need a car and a few days. **The Southern Highlands** can be explored in a day or two, best reached in a two-hour drive via the Hume Highway from Sydney; follow signs for Mittagong. There are daily train services from Sydney to the Southern Highlands (131 500) but it's hard to explore further without a car. Coach companies offer tours from Sydney.

To visit the **South Coast,** leave Sydney on the Princes Highway and follow signs for Wollongong, Kiama, Nowra, Jervis Bay, Ulladulla, Narooma, Merimbula and Eden. There are daily train services from Sydney to the South Coast (131 500) but you'll need a car to go exploring.

There are scores of accommodation options in the region from the beautiful Villa Dalmeny in Kiama (see page 124) to B&Bs. **South Coast Accommodation Services** handles 40 of the best properties and can arrange bookings, (02) 4464 2477; www.accommodationservices.com.au Visit the **Southern Highlands Visitor Information Centre,** 62-70 Main Street, Mittagong, (02) 4871 2888 or 1300 657 559, open daily, 8am-5.30pm, or the **Shoalhaven Tourist Centre,** 254 Princes Highway, Bomaderry, near Nowra, (02) 4421 0778, open daily, 9am-5pm.

If you want to explore **Morton National Park,** visit the **National Parks and Wildlife Service Visitor Centre** at Fitzroy Falls, (02) 4887 7270, open daily, 8.30am-5pm, for maps and advice. Park entry is free.

The Southern Highlands are prone to heavy **mists** at various times of year which can shroud the many views. It's wise to check weather conditions in advance of your visit.

The peaceful Southern Highlands.

Southern Highlands

There's more than a touch of England about the Southern Highlands. On a chill winter's day, when a mist hangs over the valleys, a dew covers the rolling farmlands, and wisps of woodsmoke curl from cottage chimneys, you'd be forgiven for thinking you're in the Yorkshire Dales.

The region's cool climate and fresh air made it a popular summer retreat for well-heeled 19th century Sydneysiders and while its fortunes have waxed and waned over the decades, it's still a magnet for people in search of a relaxing break from big city life.

The towns and villages in the Southern Highlands are a delight. The beautifully preserved village of Berrima, founded in 1831, is a must-see with its sandstone courthouse and gaol, village green, charming cottages and guest houses.

The village is also home to The Surveyor-General Inn (1834), the oldest continuously licensed pub in Australia, an historic Post Office and a host of art and craft galleries.

Another highlight is Bowral, nestled in the shadow of Mount Gibraltar and the commercial centre of the Southern Highlands. Founded in the 1860s, the town flourished as a retreat for wealthy Sydneysiders and a legacy of stately homes and beautiful gardens remains. The annual Tulip Time (September/October) is one of Australia's leading flower festivals.

Bowral was also the childhood home of cricket legend and national hero Sir Don Bradman. The oval is named after him and the neighbouring Bradman Museum is a fitting testament to his life and the world of cricket. There's also a pleasant self-guided Bradman

Walk around Bowral if you have the time.

Other villages include Braemar, Burrawang, Sutton Forest, Exeter and Bundanoon, which transforms itself into *Brigadoon* for an annual Highland Gathering each April, while Mittagong and Moss Vale are larger commercial centres.

Robertson, one of the locations for the hit movie *Babe*, is also home to the Yarrawa Brush Nature Reserve, a five-hectare remnant of an ancient temperate rainforest.

The most beautiful natural attraction in the Southern Highlands is Morton National Park, a majestic wilderness area boasting the spectacular Fitzroy Falls, panoramic lookouts and bushwalking trails.

The falls plunge 82 metres over a sheer-drop cliff into the Yarunga Valley and can be viewed from walking trails close to the visitor centre (see Directions).

From Fitzroy Falls you can drive through Kangaroo Valley to Nowra and Jervis Bay if you want to take in the highlands and the coast.

Directions Leave Sydney via the Hume Highway and follow signs for Mittagong. There are train services (131 500) but it's hard to explore the region without a car. South Coast Accommodation Services is on (02) 4464 2477. The Southern Highlands Visitor Information Centre, (02) 4871 2888 or (1300 657 559), is at 62-70 Main Street, Mittagong, open daily, 8am-5.30pm. If you want to explore Morton National Park, call at the National Parks and Wildlife Service Visitors Centre at Fitzroy Falls, (02) 4887 7270, open daily, 8.30am-5pm; park entry is free.

magicmoment

Standing at Fitzroy Falls as it cascades 82 metres over sheer rock into the tree-shrouded Yarunga Valley.

mustsee

The Bradman Museum, St Jude Street, Bowral, (02) 4862 1247, dedicated to cricket legend and national hero Sir Don Bradman; open daily 10am-4pm, $7 adult.

mustdo

Walk around the historic village of Berrima with its sandstone courthouse and jail, pretty cottages, arts and crafts galleries, guest houses and cafes.

Jervis Bay

50

magicmoment

Watching a Jervis Bay sunset from Hyams Beach, or neighbouring Chinaman's Beach, said to have the whitest sand in the world.

mustsee

Green Patch, on the southern shore of Jervis Bay, where you can see kangaroos and colourful birdlife at close range.

mustdo

A visit to the Kiama Blowhole, which spurts plumes of sea spray up to 60 metres high. Keep to the public footpaths.

The joy of the NSW South Coast is that you can enjoy the best of the coast and the countryside, a wild and beautiful coastline which is not only fringed with glorious beaches and pretty towns and villages but framed by the rolling hills of the Southern Highlands and bushland of the southern hinterland.

The South Coast fits into the Best-Kept Secret file because it lies off the beaten tourist track yet boasts some of the most beautiful scenery in Australia. The climate is slightly cooler than the North Coast but summer or winter, it makes for a delightful escape from Sydney.

The drive itself is pleasant, south from the city along the Princes Highway past the Royal National Park, the panoramic views of Stanwell Tops (a favourite hang-gliding spot), and alongside the industrial city of Wollongong. Soon the road skirts the coast, between the farmlands of the Southern Highlands and the sea to Kiama, the first of the coastal communities.

It's worth stopping in Kiama to see the Blowhole (see Must Do) and historic Terraces, built in 1885 to house quarry workers, now a row of shops, galleries and restaurants.

Ten kilometres inland lies the sleepy dairy village of Jamberoo and a little further on is Minnamurra, a magnificent rainforest reserve with boardwalks and two waterfalls. From Kiama, the Princes Highway leads to Berry, another leafy town with historic pubs, art and craft galleries and antiques stores, and on to the bustling Nowra.

The major attraction for this area is Jervis Bay, a vast calm-water bay several times the size of Sydney Harbour and fringed by the Jervis Bay National Park, bayside communities, campsites, caravan parks and beaches reputed to have the whitest sand in the world.

The crystal-clear waters of Jervis Bay are home to a variety of marine and birdlife, including dolphins, seals, rays, penguins and sea eagles, as well as the occasional migrating whale. Our favourite spot is Hyams Beach, and neighbouring Chinaman's Beach, with their chalk-white sands and safe swimming. There's a corner store at Hyams and houses and cabins for rent. You'll find more accommodation, shops and restaurants in nearby Huskisson and Vincentia.

Jervis Bay National Park is a short drive away and the campsite at Green Patch (see Must See) has a resident population of kangaroos. Dolphin Watch Cruises, (02) 4441 6311, operates bay tours from Huskisson.

If you want to explore further, the Princes Highway winds on to the coastal communities of Ulladulla, Batemans Bay, Narooma, Merimbula and Eden, all offering a pleasant South Coast experience.

Directions Take the Princes Highway from Sydney, via Wollongong, and follow signs for Kiama, Nowra and Jervis Bay. There are train services (131 500) but it's hard to explore the region without a car. Coach companies offer tours from Sydney. South Coast Accommodation Services, (02) 4464 2477; The Shoalhaven Tourist Centre, 254 Princes Highway, Bomaderry, near Nowra, (02) 4421 0778, is open daily, 9am-5pm.

Wish you were here? The dazzling white sands of Hyams Beach.

Aussie expressions

arvo:	afternoon	**larrikin:**	colourful character
barbie:	barbecue		
beauty!:	great	**mate:**	friend
bottle shop:	liquor store or off-licence	**middy:**	small glass of beer
bludger:	lazy person	**mozzies:**	mosquitos
brekkie:	breakfast	**no worries:**	everything's just fine
bush:	the country, wilderness	**ocker:**	loud-mouthed Australian
bush tucker:	native food		
chook:	chicken	**pokies:**	poker machines
cossie:	swimming costume	**pom:**	someone of English descent
crook:	bad, or feeling ill	**ripper!:**	fantastic
daggy:	unfashionable	**sanger:**	sandwich
dill:	idiot	**schooner:**	large glass of beer
doona:	duvet or quilt		
dunny:	toilet	**shout:**	to buy a round of drinks
esky:	ice box for drinks or food	**snag:**	sausage
fair dinkum:	honest	**stubby:**	small bottle of beer
fair go!:	give us a break		
feral:	wild	**sunnies:**	sunglasses
g'day:	good day, hello	**thongs:**	flip-flops
grog:	alcohol	**tinnie:**	can of beer
hoon:	tearaway male	**true blue:**	genuine
koori:	Aborigine	**whinger:**	moaner

simply the best

Hotels

Sydney has a wide range of accommodation to suit all tastes and budgets. Most major credit cards are accepted. Note: Accommodation in city centre hotels is subject to a 10 per cent State Government bed tax. Unless stated, breakfast is extra. Room rates quoted are full price. It is much cheaper to book an airfare and accommodation package; check also for special deals and packages which are available year-round.

LUXURY

- **Park Hyatt** 7 Hickson Road, The Rocks. Arguably the best hotel in Sydney with panoramic views of the Opera House. Double rooms from $600 a night (9256 1690); www.hyatt.com
- **Hotel Inter.Continental** 117 Macquarie Street. High-rise hotel built around the historic Treasury building. Double rooms from $385 a night (9230 0200); www.interconti.com
- **The Regent of Sydney** 199 George Street. High-rise hotel, close to Circular Quay, with views of the city and harbour. Double rooms from $375 a night (9238 0000); www.fourseasons.com
- **ANA Hotel** 176 Cumberland Street. High-rise hotel, close to Circular Quay, with city and harbour views. Double rooms from $370 a night (9250 6111); www.anahotel.com.au
- **Ritz-Carlton** 93 Macquarie Street. Club-like hotel overlooking the Botanic Gardens. Double rooms from $419 a night (9252 4600). Sister hotel Ritz-Carlton Double Bay, 33 Cross Street. Doubles from $349 (9362 4455); www.ritzcarlton.com
- **The Observatory** 89-113 Kent Street. Award-winning hotel, part of the Orient-Express Hotels group, with an excellent restaurant Galileo. Double rooms from $495 a night (9256 2222); www.observatoryhotel.com.au
- **Sheraton on the Park** 161 Elizabeth Street. Grand hotel overlooking Hyde Park and close to the city centre. Double rooms from $370 a night (9286 6000); www.sheraton.com
- **The Westin Sydney** 1 Martin Place. Landmark hotel in the centre of the city, towering over the heritage-listed General Post Office. Double rooms from $350 a night (8223 1111).

MID-RANGE

- **Novotel on Darling Harbour** 100 Murray Street, Pyrmont. Box-seat location with terrific city views. Double rooms from $235 a night (9934 0000). Novotel's Hotel Ibis (9563 0888) and Grand Mercure Apartments (9563 6666) are next door.

- **Parkroyal at Darling Harbour** 150 Day Street. Double rooms from $300 a night (9261 1188). Sister hotels: Old Sydney Parkroyal at The Rocks (9252 0524); Landmark Parkroyal Potts Point (9368 3000); Pier One Parkroyal Sydney Harbour (8298 9999). Sister hotel chains include the cheaper Centra and Travelodge; www.sphc.com.au
- **Hotel Nikko Darling Harbour** 161 Sussex Street. One of Sydney's biggest hotels, with 645 rooms, on the city side of Darling Harbour. Double rooms from $295 a night (9299 1231); www.hotelnikko.com.au
- **Renaissance** 30 Pitt Street. High-rise hotel close to Circular Quay, The Rocks and Opera House. Double rooms from $325 a night (9372 2233); www.renaissancehotels.com
- **Hilton Sydney** 259 Pitt Street. Centrally located high-rise hotel opposite the Queen Victoria Building. Double rooms from $300 a night (9266 2000); www.hilton.com
- **The Wentworth** 61-101 Phillip Street. Sydney flagship of the Rydges hotel chain in the central business district. Double rooms from $275 a night (9230 0700); www.rydges.com.au
- **All Seasons Premier Menzies** 14 Carrington Street. European-style hotel, close to all the city's major attractions. Double rooms from $300 a night (9299 1000); www.allseasons.com.au
- **Duxton Hotel** 88 Alfred Street, Milsons Point. Lower north shore location next to the Harbour Bridge. Double rooms from $265 a night (9955 1111); www.duxtonhotels.com.sg

> The NSW Travel Centre in the arrivals hall at Sydney International Airport (9667 6050) offers some of the cheapest standby hotel rates in Sydney, if you don't want to pre-book your accommodation. The centre is open daily, 6am-11.30pm, all year.

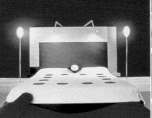

Quay West   Medusa   All Seasons Premier Menzies

CHEAPER

- **Aarons Hotel** 37 Ultimo Road, Haymarket. Excellent location, price and accommodation in the heart of Chinatown. Double rooms from $130 a night with breakfast (9281 5555).
- **Oxford Koala Hotel** cnr Oxford and Pelican streets, City. Good-value Best Western hotel and serviced apartments, easy walking distance from the city centre. Double rooms from $130 a night (9269 0645).
- **Glasgow Arms** 527 Harris Street, Ultimo. Very comfortable pub-style accommodation opposite the Powerhouse Museum and a short walk to the city centre. Double rooms from $120 a night with breakfast (9211 2354).

SERVICED APARTMENTS

- **Quay West** 98 Gloucester Street, The Rocks. High-rise apartment hotel, close to Circular Quay, with wonderful harbour views. Double rooms from $320 a night (9240 6000).
- **2 Bond Street** cnr Bond and George streets, City. Stylish executive apartment hotel. Double rooms from $280 a night (9250 9555); www.2bondst.com.au
- **Grand Esplanade** 54a West Esplanade, Manly. Modern apartment hotel, close to Manly Wharf and major attractions. Double rooms from $180 a night (9976 4600).

BOUTIQUE HOTELS

- **Medusa** 267 Darlinghurst Road, Darlinghurst. Cutting-edge luxury and sophistication in the heart of groovy Darlinghurst. Double rooms from $230 a night (9331 1000); www.medusa.com.au
- **The Russell** 143a George Street, The Rocks. Historic hotel offering charming accommodation close to Circular Quay. Double rooms from $180 a night (9241 3543).
- **Ravesi's** Campbell Parade, Bondi. Comfortable small hotel, overlooking the beach and buzzy Campbell Parade. Double rooms with a view from $140 a night (9365 4422).

GUEST HOUSES

- **Periwinkle** 18-19 East Esplanade, Manly. Charming guest house with stylish rooms, harbour views, and close to all Manly's attractions. Double rooms from $140 a night with breakfast (9977 4668).
- **Cremorne Point Manor** 6 Cremorne Road, Cremorne Point. Cheap but comfortable accommodation, walking distance from Cremorne Point Wharf. Double rooms from $95 a night (9953 7899).

YOUTH HOSTELS

- There are five youth hostels in Sydney and more than 140 in Australia, all offering cheap and comfortable accommodation. For details, contact the Youth Hostels Association, 422 Kent Street, Sydney (9261 1111), or the YHA office in your State or country; www.yha.org.au

HOME STAYS

- Bed and Breakfast Australia offers a variety of accommodation such as hosted home stays, small guest houses and boutique hotels, farm stays, home-hosted dinners, and Sydney 2000 Olympic Games accommodation. For details, contact PO Box 727, Newport, NSW 2106 (9999 0366). For pub stays, contact the Australian Hotels Association (9281 6922); www.aha-nsw.asn.au

BEYOND SYDNEY

- **Lilianfels** Lilianfels Avenue, Katoomba, Blue Mountains. Luxury hotel perched on the edge of the Jamison Valley and close to the Three Sisters. Double rooms from $305 a night, (02) 4780 1200; www.slh.com
- **Hunter Resort** Hermitage Road, Pokolbin, Hunter Valley. Award-winning motel resort set in a vineyard with its own winery and excellent restaurant. Double rooms from $140 a night, (02) 4998 7777; www.hunterresort.com.au
- **Villa Dalmeny** 72 Shoalhaven Street, Kiama. Beautiful South Coast guest house offering luxury accommodation in four themed suites. From $190 a night with breakfast, (02) 4233 1911.

Restaurants

Sydney is foodie heaven. Almost every style and nationality of cuisine is on offer in restaurants to suit all tastes and budgets from five-star gourmet to no-star BYO (bring your own wine). Most Sydney restaurants are open daily for lunch and dinner, although some close on Mondays. It's wise to make a booking for the more expensive restaurants. Most restaurants accept major credit cards. Some restaurants are fully licensed and offer wine by the bottle or glass; some are licensed and BYO; if you take your own wine, you'll be charged a nominal corkage fee. Tipping is optional. Most restaurants are relaxed and casual and offer smoking and non-smoking tables. The following is a selection of our favourite restaurants.

CIRCULAR QUAY

- **Bennelong** Sydney Opera House. One of the city's best restaurants and bars in Sydney's architectural masterpiece. Ideal for pre- or post-theatre dinner. Modern Australian, smart casual, $$$, (9250 7548).
- **Quadrant** 61 Macquarie Street. Quay Grand's signature restaurant with sparkling views over Circular Quay. Modern Australian, smart casual, $$$, (9256 4000).
- **Cafe Sydney** 31 Alfred Street. Rooftop restaurant perched on top of the historic Customs House with great harbour views. Modern Australian, smart casual, $$, (9251 8683).
- **Merrony's** 2 Albert Street. Perennial Sydney favourite owned by chef Paul Merrony on the ground floor of The Quay Apartments. Ideal for pre- or post-theatre dinner. Modern Australian, smart casual, $$, (9247 9323).

THE ROCKS

- **Rockpool** 107 George Street. Flagship restaurant of top Sydney chef Neil Perry with the emphasis on seafood. Modern Australian, smart, $$$$, (9252 1888).
- **Doyle's at the Quay** Overseas Passenger Terminal. Indoor-outdoor sister restaurant to Doyle's on the Beach at Watsons Bay. Seafood and sweeping views to the Opera House, casual, $$, (9252 3400). Suitable for children.
- **The Waterfront** Campbells Cove. Part of a complex of good Chinese, Italian and seafood restaurants with Opera House and harbour views. Seafood, casual, $$, (9247 3666). Suitable for children.
- **Phillip's Foote** 101 George Street. Popular historic pub-style restaurant with courtyard cook-it-yourself dining. Barbecue and carvery, casual, $, (9241 1485).
- **bel mondo Anti Bar** Level 3, Argyle Stores, 12-24 Argyle Street. Groovy bar and restaurant offering antipasti and other delicacies. Italian, smart casual, $$, (9241 3700).

DARLING HARBOUR

- **Ampersand** Roof Terrace, Cockle Bay Wharf. Chef Tony Bilson's international award-winning restaurant overlooking Darling Harbour. French/Australian, smart, $$$$, (9264 6666).
- **Chinta Ria** Temple of Love, Roof Terrace, Cockle Bay Wharf. Popular rooftop restaurant with indoor-outdoor dining and views over Darling Harbour. Asian, casual, $, (9264 3211). Licensed and BYO.

CITY

- **Banc** 53 Martin Place. The ultimate corporate dining room with top-drawer food, wine and service. Hang the expense, mortgage the kids, sit back and enjoy. French/European, smart, $$$$, (9233 5300).

DARLINGHURST

- **Oh, Calcutta!** 251 Victoria Street, Darlinghurst. One of Sydney's best Indian restaurants with a swag of awards to its name. Classic Indian with a modern twist, casual, $, (9360 3650). BYO.
- **Onde** 346 Liverpool Street, Darlinghurst. Groovy inner city bistro loved by the local "in" crowd. You can't book, so arrive early to guarantee a table. Modern Australian, casual, $$, (9331 8749).

KINGS CROSS

- **Bayswater Brasserie** 32 Bayswater Road, King Cross. A favourite of Sydney's social set, stylishly buzzy. Modern Australian, smart casual, $$, (9357 2177).
- **Mezzaluna** 123 Victoria Street, Potts Point. Italy meets Australia in this stylish restaurant, owned and run by the affable Polese family. Cutting-edge menus, a pleasant terrace and city skyline views. Smart casual, $$$, (9357 1988).
- **Macleay Street Bistro** 73a Macleay Street, Potts Point. Lively BYO bistro in leafy Potts Point. You can't book, so arrive early to ensure a table. Modern Australian, casual, $$, (9358 4891).

Bennelong

Sydney rock oysters

bel mondo

ON THE WATER

- **Bathers' Pavilion** 4 The Esplanade, Balmoral. Stylish restaurant, cafe and bar in the restored Bathers' Pavilion, overlooking beautiful Balmoral Beach. Modern Australian, smart casual, $ to $$$$, (9969 5050).
- **The Bower Restaurant** Marine Parade, Manly. Waterfront restaurant on the scenic Manly to Shelly Beach walk. Modern Australian, breakfast and lunch only, casual, $$, (9977 5451). BYO. Suitable for children.
- **Doyle's on the Beach** 11 Marine Parade, Watsons Bay. Fish and chips in one of the world's most beautiful settings (see page 72). Seafood, casual, $$, (9337 2007). Suitable for children.
- **The Harbour Restaurant** Northern Boardwalk, Sydney Opera House. The harbour, Opera House and good food in one package. Ideal for lunch or pre-theatre dining. Modern Australian, smart casual, $$, (9250 7191).
- **Pier** 594 New South Head Road, Rose Bay. One of Sydney's best fish restaurants with beautiful harbour views. Seafood, smart casual, $$$, (9327 6561).
- **The Cove** Manly Wharf. Pleasant and relaxed indoor-outdoor restaurant overlooking the sparkling waters of Manly Cove. Seafood, casual, $$, (9976 2400).

FOOD WITH A VIEW

- **Quay** Overseas Passenger Terminal, Circular Quay. Top-price, top-drawer restaurant with a stunning Opera House panorama. French, smart, $$$$, (9251 5600).
- **The Summit** Level 47, Australia Square, 264 George Street. The revolving restaurant is back in style. Minimalist decor allows the food and city skyline to sparkle. Classic Australian, smart casual, $$$, (9247 9777).

OUT OF THE ORDINARY

- **Edna's Table** 204 Clarence Street. For a taste of real Australia, you can't go past this stylish city centre restaurant. Crocodile, emu, kangaroo and an array of native produce, served with panache by brother-and-sister team Raymond and Jennice Kersh. Smart casual, $$$, (9267 3933).
- **GPO** 1 Martin Place, City. Complex of gourmet restaurants, bars and food stores in the newly renovated General Post Office.

WORTH A DETOUR

- **Tetsuya's** 729 Darling Street, Rozelle. Sydney's guru of gastronomy, Tetsuya Wakuda, serves dishes to-die-for in an unassuming inner west suburban terrace. Fixed-price lunch ($75) and dinner ($110), Tuesday to Friday and Saturday lunch only. Japanese/French, smart casual, (9555 1017). Licensed and BYO. Book well in advance.
- **Milsons** 17 Willoughby Street, Kirribilli. One of the best restaurants on Sydney's north shore, close to the steps onto the Harbour Bridge. Ideal for lunch or dinner. Modern Australian, smart casual, $$$, (9955 7075).
- **La Goulue** 17 Alexander Street, Crows Nest. Classic French food in a small but cosy suburban north shore restaurant. Smart casual, $$, (9439 1640). BYO.

THEMED

- **Planet Hollywood** Level 2, 600 George Street. Sydney branch of the international chain. Casual, $, (9267 7827). Suitable for children.

If you want to know more, The Sydney Morning Herald's Good Food Guide is available at bookstores and newsagencies, RRP $19.95.

PRICE CODE: Three courses without wine: $ (up to $35 a person) • $$ ($35-$50) • $$$ ($50-$75) • $$$$ (over $75) Fully licensed unless otherwise stated.

Cafes

One thing is for certain in Sydney; you'll never be far from a good coffee. Some of the city's best cafes are in Darlinghurst and Potts Point (next to Kings Cross in Sydney's inner east) where coffee-drinking is an art form but there are decent cafes throughout the city. Many serve breakfast and lunch and are open throughout the day.

- **MCA Cafe** Good coffee and great views to Circular Quay and the Opera House from the sun-drenched verandah of the Museum of Contemporary Art, 140 George Street, The Rocks (9241 4253).
- **Hyde Park Barracks** Pleasant retreat from the city crowds offering coffee and lunch in the gravelled courtyard of the historic Hyde Park Barracks, southern end of Macquarie Street (9223 1155).
- **bills** Rub shoulders with the groovy Darlinghurst set at this simple but classic cafe in a restored Victorian corner house. White walls, wood tables, good coffee. 433 Liverpool Street, Darlinghurst (9360 9631).
- **Cafe Dov** Cool and classic corner cafe with sandstone walls, wood floors and pavement dining. Popular with local art students and the Darlinghurst intelligentsia. 252 Forbes Street, Darlinghurst (9360 9594).
- **Bar Coluzzi** Legendary cafe run by the affable Luigi Coluzzi for 40 years. It's little more than a hole in the wall decorated with family memorabilia, pavement stools and a buzzy atmosphere. 322 Victoria Street, Darlinghurst (9380 5420).
- **Parmalat** Next door to Bar Coluzzi but light years away in design. Narrow galley-style cafe spills onto Victoria Street where you can watch the passing parade. 320b Victoria Street, Darlinghurst (9331 2914).
- **Tropicana** Another popular city cafe with a bit more room to move. Stainless steel tables, pavement seating, efficient service and an attitude to match. 227b Victoria Street, Darlinghurst (9360 9809).
- **La Buvette** Nestled in leafy Potts Point, this tiny cafe more than holds its own in the coffee and food stakes. It's at the Macleay Street end of Challis Avenue, Potts Point (9358 5113).
- **Spring** Next door to La Buvette but very different in style with a shiny white decor and pavement tables. Drop-dead groovy with great coffee to boot. Macleay Street end of Challis Avenue (9331 0190).

- **Vaucluse House Tearooms** Cafe-cum-bistro with a country atmosphere in the grounds of historic Vaucluse House. It's especially lively at weekends, with offerings from scones and tea to tuna salad (9388 8188).

COFFEES

- **Espresso/Short Black:** Small shot of black coffee.
- **Long Black:** Larger serve of black coffee.
- **Macchiato:** Espresso with a dash of hot foamed milk.
- **Cappucino:** One-third espresso, one-third hot steamed milk, one-third frothed milk.
- **Flat White:** Half a cup of espresso, topped with hot milk.
- **Cafe Latte:** One-quarter espresso, three-quarters creamy hot milk, topped with foamed milk.
- **Mocha:** One-third espresso, two-thirds frothed milk with chocolate syrup.
- **Vienna Coffee:** Double espresso topped with whipped cream and chocolate dusting.
- **Cafe Freddo:** Freshly made espresso cooled in the fridge.
- **Ristretto:** Traditional Italian small pour of espresso. Coffee can be also ordered with soy or skimmed milk and decaffeinated coffee.

Shopping and Aboriginal Art

Most shops are open weekdays, 9am-5.30pm, with late-night shopping on Thursday to 9pm. Shops are open Saturday, 9am-4pm, and many trade on Sunday. Major credit cards are accepted in most stores. There are two annual sale times, immediately after Christmas from December 26 and during July after the end of the financial year.

CITY CENTRE

- **Pitt Street Mall** Pedestrian shopping mall home to seven arcades: Sydney Central Plaza, Centrepoint, Imperial, Mid City Centre, Strand Arcade, Skygarden, Glasshouse.
- **George Street** The main commercial street running the length of the central business district from The Rocks to Central Station. George Street is lined with banks, shops, department stores, cinemas, restaurants and cafes.
- **The Rocks** Home to a variety of quality stores, galleries, duty-free shops, opal stores and Australian arts and crafts. The Argyle Stores, 12-24 Argyle Street, is especially good.
- **Harbourside** Refurbished shopping centre at Darling Harbour boasting some excellent new outlets like The Cotton Store and Gavala Aboriginal Cultural Centre.
- **King and Castlereagh Streets** Lined with chic designer emporiums from Chanel to Gucci and Hermes.
- **Queen Victoria Building** One of the most beautiful shopping arcades in Sydney with 200 quality stores over four levels. The historic building is worth seeing even if you don't buy anything. Bounded by George, Market, Druitt and York streets (9264 9209).
- **MLC Centre** Upmarket shopping centre, corner of King and Castlereagh streets. The historic GPO hotel and restaurant complex is nearby in Martin Place.
- **Chifley Plaza** The world's top names – Gucci, Cartier, Tiffany, MaxMara, Kenzo and Moschino – in one elegant centre in Chifley Square.
- **Grace Bros** A Sydney retail institution (part of Pitt Street Mall) which has undergone a multi-million-dollar makeover (9238 9111).
- **David Jones** There's no other store like David Jones (or so says the advertising slogan) but you can judge for yourself. Twin department stores on the corner of Elizabeth and Market streets (9266 5544).

- **Gowings** Legendary menswear store with something for the man who has (almost) everything. 319 George Street, Wynyard (9262 1281). The main Gowings is on the corner of George and Market streets (9264 6321).

SUBURBAN SHOPPING MALLS

- **Bondi Junction Plaza, Chatswood Chase, Penrith Plaza, Westfield** Chatswood, Miranda and Parramatta.

DUTY-FREE

- **Downtown** Strand Arcade, City (9233 3166).
- **Allders** 22 Pitt Street, City (9241 5844).

ABORIGINAL ART

- **Gavala Aboriginal Cultural Centre** Sydney's only Aboriginal-owned and operated cultural centre. Authentic artwork, music, books, performances and art appreciation talks. Harbourside Darling Harbour (9212 7232).
- **Djamu Gallery** Displaying and selling a range of quality Aboriginal, Torres Strait Islander and Pacific islands artworks and artefacts in a stylish gallery at Customs House in Customs Square. There are permanent and changing exhibitions. 31, Alfred Street, Circular Quay (9320 6429).
- **Yiribana** Art Gallery of NSW (see page 23).
- **Jinta Desert Art** One of Australia's largest collections of Aboriginal art by leading artists from Central Australia. 154-156 Clarence Street (9290 3639).
- **Boomalli Aboriginal Artists Co-op** Home to some of the best authentic Aboriginal artwork in Australia. Check for exhibitions. 191 Parramatta Road, Annandale (9698 2047).
- **Northern Territory and Outback Centre** Formerly the National Aboriginal Cultural Centre, with a range of artworks and artefacts for sale. Shop 28, 1-25 Harbour Street, Darling Harbour (9283 7477).

Entertainment

SYDNEY OPERA HOUSE
- **Opera Australia**
  Winter season: June to November
  Summer season: January to March
- **Sydney Symphony Orchestra**
  Season: February to November
- **Australian Chamber Orchestra**
  Season: February to November
- **Australian Ballet**
  Seasons: March to May
  November and December
- **Sydney Theatre Company**
  Season: All year
- **The Studio**
  Season: All year
  Comedy to jazz and cabaret
- **Sydney Opera House**
  Box Office (9250 7777)

CONCERTS
- **Sydney Entertainment Centre**
  Harbour Street, Haymarket
  Ticketek (9266 4800)
- **Star City Casino Showroom**
  80 Pyrmont Street, Pyrmont
  (9777 9000)
- **Sydney Town Hall**
  Cnr George and Druitt streets,
  City (9265 9007)
- **City Recital Hall**
  Angel Place, City (9899 2488)
- **Free outdoor concerts**
  Weekdays in the Martin
  Place amphitheatre

CITY CENTRE CINEMAS
- **Greater Union**
  525 George Street (9267 8666)
- **Hoyts**
  505 George Street (9273 7431)
- **Village**
  545 George Street (9264 6701)
- Check newspapers for screenings
  and independent cinema listings.

THEATRE
MUSICALS AND
MAJOR PRODUCTIONS:
- **Capitol Theatre**
  13 Campbell Street,
  Haymarket (9320 5000)
- **State Theatre**
  49 Market Street, City (9373 6655)
- **Lyric Theatre**
  Star City, 80 Pyrmont Street,
  Pyrmont (9657 8500)

- **Her Majesty's Theatre**
  107 Quay Street, near Railway
  Square, City (9212 3411)
- **Theatre Royal**
  MLC Centre, King Street, City
  (9320 9191)

PLAYS:
- **Wharf Theatre**, home of the
  Sydney Theatre Company,
  Pier 4, Hickson Road, Walsh Bay
  (9250 1777)
- **Belvoir Street Theatre**
  25 Belvoir Street, Surry Hills
  (9699 3444)
- **Ensemble Theatre**
  78 McDougall Street,
  Milsons Point (9929 0644)

DANCE
- **Sydney Dance Company**
  Pier 4, Hickson Road,
  Walsh Bay (9221 4811)
- **Bangarra Dance Theatre**
  Traditional and contemporary
  Aboriginal dance and music,
  mainly touring (9251 5333)

COMEDY
- **Harold Park Hotel**
  115 Wigram Road, Glebe
  (9692 0564)
- **Comedy Store**
  Fox Studios Australia, Moore Park
  (1300 369 849)

CASINO
- **Star City**
  80 Pyrmont Street, Pyrmont
  (9777 9000)

PUBS AND BARS
- **Hero of Waterloo**
  81 Lower Fort Street, The Rocks
  (9252 4553) Historic and lively
- **Lord Nelson**
  Cnr Kent and Argyle streets,
  The Rocks (9251 4044)
  Cold beer and history
- **Orient Hotel**
  89 George Street, The Rocks
  (9251 1255) Loud and lively
- **Soho Bar and Lounge**
  171 Victoria Street,
  Potts Point (9358 6511)
  Groovers and shakers

- **Slip Inn**
  111 Sussex Street (9299 4777)
  Pool bar and restaurant
- **CBD Hotel**
  75 York Street, (9299 8292)
  Stylish bars, excellent restaurant
- **Horizon's Bar**
  Level 36, ANA Hotel,
  176 Cumberland Street,
  The Rocks (9250 6000)
  Cocktails in the clouds
- **International**
  Top of the Town Hotel
  227 Victoria Street,
  Darlinghurst (9360 9080)
  Cool people, cool view
- **Wine Banc**
  53 Martin Place (9233 5399)
  Subterranean sophistication

NIGHTCLUBS
- **Grand Pacific Blue Room**
  Cnr Oxford and
  South Dowling streets,
  Paddington (9331 7108)
  As cool as they come
- **Embassy**
  16-18 Cross Street,
  Double Bay (9328 2200)
  Sydney's party crowd
- **Home**
  Southern End Cockle Bay Wharf
  (9266 0600) Loud and groovy

JAZZ
- **Strawberry Hills Hotel**
  453 Elizabeth Street, Surry Hills
  (9698 2997)
- **Harbourside Brasserie**
  Pier 1, Hickson Road, The Rocks
  (9252 3000)
- **The Basement**
  29 Reiby Place, City (9251 2797)
- **Soup Plus**
  383 George Street, City (9299 7728)
- **Orient Hotel**
  89 George Street,
  The Rocks (9251 1255)

TICKET AGENCIES
- **Ticketmaster** (9320 9000)
- **Ticketek** (9266 4800)
- **For Entertainment listings**,
  see Metro in Friday's Sydney
  Morning Herald.

Family Fun

- **Sydney Aquarium**
  One of Sydney's best attractions, part of the Darling Harbour complex. Underwater walking tunnels, Great Barrier Reef display, Touch and Learn Pool, and more than 5,000 sea creatures including sharks, stingrays, seals and saltwater crocodiles. It's open daily (9262 2300), 9.30am-10pm, $17.50 adult, $8 child, family pass from $23.50 (see page 32).

- **Sega World**
  Indoor theme park, part of the Darling Harbour complex. Rides, games and more. It's at 25 Darling Street (behind the Panasonic IMAX Theatre), various daily opening times, $28 adult ($22 if accompanying a child), child prices vary to $22 (9273 9273).

- **Cook and Phillip Park**
  Major aquatic and recreation centre in the heart of the city, next to St Mary's Cathedral, College Street. Facilities include a 50m pool, fitness centre, hydrotherapy pool and wave pool. It's open Monday to Friday 6am-10pm, Saturday 7am-7pm, Sunday 7am-9pm, entry $4 (9326 0444).

- **Taronga Zoo**
  One of the world's great zoos with magnificent views of Sydney Harbour (see page 52).

- **Fox Studios Australia**
  Dubbed Hollywood on the Harbour, it's a working film and television studio as well as a major public entertainment complex with self-guided backlot tours into a world of animation, make-up, costume, special effects, sound and live performances. The main Bent Street offers music, comedy and performances, 16 cinemas, shopping and dining. The backlot tours operate daily 10am-6pm (closed Christmas Day), $37.95 adult, $22.95 child. Bent Street is open daily 10am to midnight, admission free. Fox Studios Australia is located at Moore Park (1300 369 849).

- **Old Sydney Town**
  A re-creation of Sydney as it was between 1788 and 1810, complete with soldiers, cannon fire, pistol duels, a trial, rides, stories and souvenirs. It's about an hour by car north of Sydney (via the F3 Freeway) at Somersby. Australian Pacific Tours (131 304), AAT Kings (9252 2788), Sydney Day Tours (9251 6101), and Gray Line (9252 4499) can take you there. It's open Wednesday to Sunday, 10am-4pm, daily during school holidays and public holidays (except Christmas Day), $18 adult, $10.50 child, (02) 4340 1104.

- **Koala Park**
  Koalas are the highlight of this park but there are many more Australian animals and birds to enjoy amid rainforest, eucalypts and native gardens. Sydney Day Tours (9251 6101) can take you there. It's at 84 Castle Hill Road, West Pennant Hills, open daily, 9am-5pm (except Christmas Day), $10 adult, $5 child (9484 3141).

- **Wonderland Sydney**
  Sydney's leading fun park with themed rides, Australian Wildlife Park, Outback Woolshed and a host of other attractions. It's about 45 minutes by car west of Sydney (via the M4 Motorway) but AAT Kings (9252 2788), Australian Pacific (131 304), Gray Line (9252 4499), and Great Sights (9241 2294) offer tours. It's open daily, 10am-5pm (except Christmas Day), $37 adult, $26-$37 child (9830 9100).

- **Featherdale Wildlife Park**
  One of Australia's largest private collections of native animals, including koalas, kangaroos, emus and wallabies, in a bush setting. It's about one hour by car west of Sydney, near Blacktown (via the M4 Motorway). Tranquillity Tours, (02) 4736 7760, offers half-day tours with pick-ups from central Sydney hotels. The park is open daily, 9am-5pm (except Christmas Day), $12 adult, $6 child (9622 1644).

- **Australian Reptile Park**
  Close to Old Sydney Town. It's a reptile park and wildlife sanctuary with many other attractions. See Old Sydney Town for tour operators. It's on the Pacific Highway at Somersby, open daily, 9am-5pm (except Christmas Day), $11.95 adult, $5.95 child, (02) 4340 1146.

- Some of Sydney's museums are also ideal for children (see page 133).

Historic Houses

Elizabeth Bay House

- **Government House (1845)**
  Until recently home to successive State Governors, the Gothic Revival mansion in Sydney's Domain is now open to the public. Explore the State Rooms and English-style gardens with their pleasant harbour views. The house is open Friday to Sunday 10am-3pm, grounds daily 10am-4pm (closed Christmas Day and Good Friday). Admission free, enter via Macquarie Street (9931 5222).

- **Old Government House (1799)**
  The oldest government building in Australia, built for Governor John Hunter on the site of Governor Arthur Phillip's house, and completed by Governor Lachlan Macquarie in 1815. It's a National Trust property in Parramatta Regional Park (9635 8149), open weekdays 10am-4pm, weekends 11am-4pm (closed Christmas Day and Good Friday).

- **Elizabeth Bay House (1839)**
  Designed for Colonial Secretary Alexander Macleay and his family, Elizabeth Bay House is a fine example of 19th century architecture in a magnificent setting overlooking Sydney Harbour. It's located at 7 Onslow Avenue, Elizabeth Bay (9356 3022), open Tuesday to Sunday 10am-4.30pm (closed Christmas Day and Good Friday). It's stop 10 on the red Sydney Explorer bus.

- **Vaucluse House (1827)**
  The home of William Charles Wentworth, father of the Australian Constitution, and his family, Vaucluse House is a Gothic-style mansion set in a harbourside estate with pretty gardens (see page 71). It's in Wentworth Road, Vaucluse (9388 7922), open Tuesday to Sunday 10am-4.30pm (closed Christmas Day and Good Friday). It's stop 9 on the blue Bondi & Bay Explorer bus.

- **Susannah Place (1844)**
  A row of four terrace houses in the heart of The Rocks providing an evocative picture of inner city Sydney life in the 19th century. It also has a delightful corner store (see page 15). It's at 58-64 Gloucester Street (9241 1893), open weekends 10am-5pm, daily during January (closed Christmas Day and Good Friday).

- **Elizabeth Farm (1793)**
  One of Sydney's most charming historic houses, once home to wool pioneers John and Elizabeth Macarthur, and Australia's oldest colonial building with shady verandahs, fine furniture and pretty gardens. It's at 70 Alice Street, Rosehill, near Parramatta (9635 9488), open daily 10am-5pm (except Christmas Day and Good Friday).

- **Rouse Hill House (1818)**
  This fragile historic house and garden resonates with almost two centuries of the Rouse family's continuous occupation. It's on Guntawong Road, Rouse Hill, a 40-minute drive north-west of Sydney, open Thursday and Sunday for guided tours only, 10am-4pm (except Christmas Day and Good Friday). Bookings required (9627 6777).

- Wheelchair access at some historic houses is limited. Check in advance for facilities.

All the historic houses mentioned (except Old Government House in Parramatta) are part of the Historic Houses Trust of New South Wales. Individual museum entry is: $6 adult, $3 child, $15 family but a better deal is the **Ticket Through Time** which allows entry to all 11 properties (including the Museum of Sydney, Hyde Park Barracks, Justice and Police Museum, Rose Seidler House, and Meroogal in Kiama). The cost is $18 adult, $10 child, $35 family, and is valid for three months from the first date of use. The ticket can be bought from any Trust property. Details (9692 8366); Infoline (1300 653 777); www.hht.nsw.gov.au

Museums

- **Australian Museum**
  One of the world's great natural history museums with permanent and changing exhibitions. It's a fascinating place to spend a morning or afternoon and is especially good for children. The museum is at 6 College Street, City (9320 6000), open daily, 9.30am-5pm (except Christmas Day), $5 adult, $2 child. It's stop 15 on the red Sydney Explorer bus.

- **Museum of Sydney**
  A modern museum built on the site of the first Government House, it explores the worlds of colonial and contemporary Sydney through objects, pictures, stories and digital-media technologies. It's on the corner of Phillip and Bridge streets, City (9251 5988), open daily, 9.30am-5pm (except Christmas Day and Good Friday), $6 adult. It's near stop 3 on the red Sydney Explorer bus.

- **Hyde Park Barracks**
  One of Sydney's finest historic buildings. Designed by colonial architect Francis Greenway in 1817 to house convicts, the classic Georgian building is now a museum tracing Sydney's often brutal colonial history. It's at the southern end of Macquarie Street, City (9223 8922), open daily, 9.30am-5pm (except Christmas Day and Good Friday), $6 adult, $15 family pass. It's near stop 4 on the red Sydney Explorer bus.

- **Sydney Jewish Museum**
  Dedicated to documenting and teaching the history of the Holocaust. Housed in the historic Maccabean Hall, the museum presents visitors with a moving critique of the best and worst of humanity. It's located at 148 Darlinghurst Road, Darlinghurst (9360 7999), open Monday to Thursday, 10am-4pm, Friday 10am-2pm, Sunday 11am-5pm, closed Saturday and Jewish holidays, $6 adult, $15 family pass.

- **Powerhouse Museum**
  Australia's largest and most popular museum, exploring aspects of human creativity from science and technology to social history, space exploration, decorative arts and design. It's especially good for children. The museum is at 500 Harris Street, Ultimo (9217 0111), behind Darling Harbour, open daily, 10am-5pm (except Christmas Day), $8 adult, $2 child, $18 family pass (best access is via the footbridge from Haymarket monorail station).

- **National Maritime Museum**
  An interactive museum tracing Australia's rich and colourful maritime history with hands-on exhibits, a cinema, computer games and a Navy gunship and submarine to explore. It's on the west bank of Darling Harbour (9298 3777), open daily, 9.30am-5pm (closed Christmas Day). Big Ticket pass to museum and vessels costs $15 adult, $5 child; a family pass costs $34. It's stop 19 on the red Sydney Explorer bus.

- **Quarantine Station, Manly**
  Hundreds of thousands of migrants arriving by ship between 1832 and the 1960s were housed here for their first few months to protect Sydney from diseases such as smallpox and influenza. More than 500 people died here. The hospital and accommodation buildings survive, a poignant reminder of Sydney's migrant heritage.
  Guided day tours operate at 1.10pm on Monday, Wednesday, Friday and weekends, last about two hours and cost $10 a person. Evening "ghost" tours operate on Wednesday, Friday and weekends, last about three hours and cost $20 a person with supper. Bookings essential. The Quarantine Station (9977 6522) is on North Head, near Manly (see page 58).

National Maritime Museum

Powerhouse Museum

Tours

COACH OPERATORS

Several coach companies offer day tours of Sydney and beyond to the Blue Mountains, Jenolan Caves, Hunter Valley, Port Stephens, South Coast and Southern Highlands, Hawkesbury River, Canberra, Homebush Bay Olympic site and other destinations. Some offer 4WD and horse-riding options:

- **AAT Kings** (9252 2788)
- **Australian Pacific Tours** (131 304)
- **Gray Line** (9252 4499)
- **Sydney Day Tours** (9251 6101)
- **Great Sights** (9241 2294)
- **Murrays Australia** (132 251)

PERSONALISED TOURS

- **Australian Wild Escapes** offers a personalised service with small-group 4WD adventure tours to the Blue Mountains, Hunter Valley, South Coast and Southern Highlands, Olympic site and city tours. The tours are day-long, all-inclusive and cost about $199 a person. Bookings (9482 8888).
- **Sydney Aboriginal Discoveries** is a 100 per cent Aboriginal-owned and operated tour company offering harbour cruises and land tours showing Sydney from the Aboriginal cultural perspective. The tour company offers indigenous food experiences, picnics and boat trips.
  The tours operate with a minimum six people; bookings (9368 7684).
- **Showing You Sydney** offers customised itineraries and tours in and around Sydney with you deciding where and when you want to go.
  Sue and Ken Moffitt offer a relaxed and personal service whether you have an hour or a week to see Sydney. Prices vary according to itinerary. Bookings (9415 1759); info@showsydney.com.au
- **Sydney Guided Tours**, run by historian, tutor and former radio and TV presenter Maureen Fry, offers personalised walking, limousine or coach tours in and around the city as well as the Southern Highlands. Prices vary according to itinerary. Bookings (9660 7157); mpfry@ozemail.com.au

UNUSUAL TOURS

- **Sydney Harbour Seaplanes**, flightseeing tours in and around Sydney (1800 803 558). Harbour scenic flights from $50 a person.
- **East Coast Motorcycle Tours**, in and around Sydney on the back of a Harley-Davidson (9555 2700). One-hour city rides from $80 a person.
- **Heli-Aust** flights and tours, 15- to 20-minute scenic harbour flights from $99 a person (9317 3402).

Terrace Falls, Blue Mountains

- **Aussie Duck,** the world's first purpose-built amphibious passenger craft which tours Sydney on land and water, 90-minute city tours, $45 adult, $25 child, $120 per family of four (131 007).
- **Unseen Sydney** offers History, Convicts and Murder Most Foul 90-minute evening walking tours of The Rocks, $17 a person (9555 2700).

HARBOUR CRUISES

- **Captain Cook Cruises,** Sydney's leading cruise operator (9206 1111)
- **Sail Venture Cruises,** luxury catamaran cruises (9262 3595)
- **Matilda Cruises,** various harbour cruises (9264 7377)
- **Bounty Cruises,** on the replica of the Bounty (9247 1789)
- **Sydney Showboats,** paddlesteamer cabaret cruises (9552 2722)
- **Vagabond Cruises,** various harbour cruises (9660 0388)
- **Harbour yacht cruises:** Sunsail (9955 6400), EastSail (9327 1166), Sydney by Sail (9280 1110).

TOUR SPECIALIST

- **Australian Travel Specialist (ATS)** is one of Sydney's leading booking agents representing all major tour operators. The service is free, operating 24 hours a day. Explore Sydney and Beyond, ATS's complete sightseeing and cruise guide detailing the full range of tours, is available from five city travel centres. Bookings (9555 2700).

SCENIC TOURS

- **National Parks and Wildlife Service** offers a range of tours to Sydney Harbour National Park, Botany Bay National Park and Sydney Harbour islands. Brochures are available from any NPWS office. General enquiries (1300 361 967), weekdays 9am-5pm.

Walks & Photo Opportunities

CITY
- **Harbour Bridge**, cross the bridge in either direction via steps in Cumberland Street, The Rocks, or on the northside by Milsons Point Station, Kirribilli. You can climb into the south-eastern pylon (200 steps) for panoramic city and harbour views and a museum on the bridge's history (see page 10).
Walk time: about 30 minutes one-way.
- **The Rocks**, a self-guided or guided walk through the maze of historic streets and alleyways (see page 15).
Walk time: minimum 2 hours.
- **Circular Quay to the Opera House, Royal Botanic Gardens and Mrs Macquarie's Chair** (see page 17). The Writers' Walk, along East Circular Quay, features a series of floor plaques dedicated to people who have contributed to Australian literature.
Walk time: about an hour one-way.
- **Sculpture Walk**, self-guided tour of the city's $4 million outdoor artwork. Maps are available from the Art Gallery of NSW and City information kiosks at Circular Quay, Martin Place and next to Sydney Town Hall, George Street. Walk time: 2-3 hours.

NORTH
- **Lavender Bay**, one of the prettiest walks in Sydney from Milsons Point Wharf, beneath the Harbour Bridge, along the wooden boardwalk past Luna Park, and around Lavender Bay. It's especially pretty at sunset (see page 49). Walk time: 30 minutes one-way.
- **Cremorne Point,** another beautiful walk from Cremorne Point Wharf around to Mosman Bay (see page 50). Walk time: 45 minutes one-way.
- **Spit to Manly,** a spectacular 10km walk through Sydney Harbour National Park with breathtaking views of the harbour (see page 57).
Walk time: 3-4 hours one-way.
- **Fairy Bower,** a delightful stroll from Manly to Shelly Beach with panoramic views to the northern beaches (see page 58). Walk time: 20 minutes one-way.
- **The Basin Trail,** a steep uphill walk to ancient Aboriginal rock art engravings in Ku-ring-gai National Park (see page 62). Walk time: 45 minutes one-way.

EAST
- **South Head,** a bracing headland walk from Camp Cove at Watsons Bay to Hornby Lighthouse on the tip of South Head (see page 72).
Walk time: 25 minutes one-way.
- **Bondi to Bronte,** a delightful clifftop walk (see page 75). Walk time: 45 minutes one-way.

OTHER OPTIONS
- **National Parks and Wildlife Service** (9585 6333): 10 Great Walks Around Sydney brochure, free from any NPWS office.
- **Historic Houses Trust of New South Wales** (1300 653 777): Take A Sydney Stroll map, free from any Trust attraction.
- **Sydney Ferries** (131 500): Go Walkabout with Sydney Ferries map, free from the Ferry Information Office, opposite Wharf 4, Circular Quay.
- **Walking Sydney**, a guide to Sydney's 25 best walks, Pan Macmillan, $14.95, from bookstores.

PHOTO OPPORTUNITIES
- Open-air lookout on top of the south-eastern pylon of the Harbour Bridge. Fabulous views of the city, Opera House and main harbour.
- The deck of any harbour ferry or cruiser.
- Bradfield Park, Kirribilli, beneath the Harbour Bridge, for city, Opera House and bridge views.
- Cremorne Point Wharf for harbour panoramas.
- Mrs Macquarie's Point in the Royal Botanic Gardens for spectacular city, Harbour Bridge, Opera House and main harbour panorama.
- Observation deck of AMP Tower (Centrepoint).
- Dobroyd Head on the Spit to Manly Walk.

Calendar of Events

JANUARY
- **Concerts in the Domain,** a series of free opera, jazz, symphony and country music concerts each Saturday evening. A Sydney institution; take a picnic.
- **Test Cricket,** Sydney Cricket Ground.
- **Sydney Festival,** the city's biggest annual arts festival. See city newspapers for programs and events.
- **Australia Day** (January 26), an array of ceremonies, concerts and colourful events, including the Sydney Harbour Ferrython and Tall Ships Parade.

FEBRUARY
- **Chinese New Year,** highlight of the Chinese calendar with lion dances, firecrackers and other celebrations.
- **Gay and Lesbian Mardi Gras Festival,** Sydney's biggest and most colourful event, a month-long festival culminating in the Gay and Lesbian Mardi Gras Parade (last Saturday in February or first Saturday in March).

MARCH
- **St Patrick's Day,** annual celebration of all things Irish.
- **Dragon Boat Races Festival,** brightly coloured long-boats vie for honours in Darling Harbour.
- **Autumn Racing Carnival,** a highlight of Sydney's racing and social calendar at Royal Randwick and Rosehill racecourses.

APRIL
- **Royal Easter Show,** annual celebration when the country comes to the city. Starts a week before Good Friday with a parade of livestock through the city centre followed by events and competitions at the Sydney Showground, Homebush Bay.
- **Anzac Day,** dawn remembrance service at the Cenotaph, Martin Place, followed by a parade of war veterans along George Street.

MAY
- **Australian Fashion Week,** revealing the latest designs.

JUNE
- **A Taste of Manly,** annual food and wine festival.
- **Sydney Film Festival,** annual showcase of local and international films at the State Theatre.
- **Darling Harbour Winter Music Festival,** music, food and fun.
- **Feast of Sydney,** annual two-week food and wine festival.

JULY
- **Yulefest,** a two-month winter celebration of Christmas in the middle of the year in the Blue Mountains.
- **Sydney Boat Show,** annual exhibition of the latest in design and technology at Darling Harbour.

AUGUST
- **City to Surf Fun Run,** one of Sydney's biggest public sporting events with tens of thousands of people competing in a road race from the city to Bondi.

SEPTEMBER
- **David Jones Spring Flower Show,** the Elizabeth Street city store blooming with colour.
- **Spring Racing Carnival,** another highlight of the Sydney racing calendar at Randwick and Rosehill.
- **Rugby League Grand Final,** the Superbowl of Australian football at Stadium Australia.
- **Sydney 2000 Olympic Games,** September 15 to October 1, at Homebush Bay, followed by the
- **Paralympic Games,** October 18-29.

OCTOBER
- **Manly Jazz Festival,** music by the beach.
- **Australian International Motor Show,** showcasing the latest in design and technology at Darling Harbour.

NOVEMBER
- **Melbourne Cup,** the highlight of Australia's racing and social calendar (at Melbourne's Flemington Racecourse) when all Australia comes to a halt.

DECEMBER
- **Carols in the Domain,** free public concert celebrating the spirit of Christmas.
- **Sydney to Hobart Yacht Race,** one of the world's toughest yacht races, departs Sydney Harbour on Boxing Day.
- **New Year's Eve,** annual celebration of fireworks over Sydney Harbour.

PUBLIC HOLIDAYS
- **New Year's Day:** January 1
- **Australia Day:** January 26
- **Good Friday** (varies)
- **Easter Monday** (varies)
- **Anzac Day:** April 25
- **Queen's Birthday:** Second Monday in June
- **Bank Holiday:** First Monday in August
- **Labour Day:** First Monday in October
- **Christmas Day:** December 25
- **Boxing Day:** December 26

Beaches and Surf Safety

Sydney is blessed with magnificent beaches, most within easy reach of the city by car or public transport. This is our choice of the best and most beautiful.

NORTHERN BEACHES

- **Palm Beach,** a gorgeous crescent of sand framed by some of Sydney's most expensive holiday homes (see page 62).
- **Whale Beach,** more beautiful weekend and holiday homes cascading down to a delightful beach.
- **Avalon Beach,** the beach which said "no" to Baywatch. Local community fought – and won – to stop the US TV series basing itself at Avalon.
- **Freshwater Beach,** another lovely beach, just north of Manly, with gently sloping shallows and crystal-clear water.
- **Manly Beach,** one of Sydney's most popular beaches, a long strip of sand framed by historic Norfolk pines (see page 58).
- **Shelly Beach,** a pretty calm-water bay facing west, ideal for swimming, snorkelling and a beach barbecue or picnic.
- **Balmoral Beach,** two beautiful harbour beaches fringing one of Sydney's most glamorous suburbs. Safe swimming, parklands and restaurants (see page 54).

EASTERN SUBURBS

- **Shark Beach,** pretty harbour beach in Nielsen Park with beautiful harbour views, ideal for swimming and a picnic (see page 71).
- **Watsons Bay,** another Sydney institution, not so much the harbour beach but the legendary Doyle's restaurant alongside (see page 72).
- **Bondi Beach,** an Australian icon (see page 75).
- **Bronte Beach,** another very pleasant beach with parklands for picnics.
- **Coogee Beach,** a family-oriented, flat-water beach which is great for swimming and picnics (see page 76).

SOUTH SYDNEY

- **South Cronulla Beach,** popular with families and swimmers.
- **Jibbon Beach,** a beautiful calm-water beach far from the crowds of the city beaches (see page 94).

SURF AND SUN SAFETY

- Always swim or surf at places patrolled by surf lifesavers or lifeguards.
- Swim ONLY between the red-and-yellow patrol flags. They mark the safest area of the beach to swim.
- Take the time to read and obey safety signs.
- Always wait about 30 minutes after a meal before swimming.
- Do not swim under the influence of alcohol or drugs.
- If you are unsure about surf conditions, ask a surf lifesaver before entering the water.
- Never run or dive into the water. Even if you checked before, conditions can change quickly.
- Beware surfboards and bodyboards.
- If you get into trouble in the water, STAY CALM. Raise your arm to signal for help, float and wait for assistance.
- Float with a current or rip. Don't try to swim against it. Float and wait for assistance.
- Respect the surf. It is a powerful and unpredictable force.
- Australia has the world's highest incidence of skin cancer. Always protect yourself at the beach with a high-factor sunblock (cover yourself regularly, especially when swimming) and a broad-brimmed hat. Take special care to protect children from the sun's harmful rays.
- Sydney beaches occasionally attract bluebottles and other stinging jellyfish. Watch for warning signs and do not swim if they are about. If stung, get immediate treatment from a surf lifesaver.
- **Surf Lifesaving Australia (9597 5588)**.

Markets and Eat Streets

MARKETS

- **Paddington**
One of Sydney's most popular markets, with an array of quality goods, fashion, arts and crafts, bargain buys and colourful entertainment. It's on the corner of Oxford and Newcombe streets, open Saturday, 10am-4pm (9331 2646).

- **The Rocks**
A Sydney weekend institution at the northern end of George Street (under the Harbour Bridge) every Saturday and Sunday with scores of street stalls selling some of the best arts and crafts in the city, 10am-5pm (9255 1717).

- **Paddy's**
The red-brick market in the heart of Chinatown is synonymous with bargain-hunting. It's on the corner of Hay and Thomas streets, near the Sydney Entertainment Centre, open Friday and weekends, 9am-4.30pm (1300 361 589).

- **Balmain**
Lively Saturday market in the grounds of St Andrew's Church, Darling Street, selling a variety of goods from children's clothes to second-hand books and antique jewellery, open 8am-4pm (0418 765 736).

- **Bondi**
Browse through racks of funky clothes, exotic plants, glassware and tourist souvenirs. It's at Bondi Beach Public School, Campbell Parade, open Sunday, 10am-5pm in summer, 4pm in winter (9315 8988).

- **Sydney Opera House**
This all-day Sunday market, on the western boardwalk of the Opera House, is great for tourists because it sells quality hand-made goods and souvenirs in a marvellous setting, open 10am-sunset.

EAT STREETS

- **King Street, Newtown:** more than 60 restaurants offering 25 ethnic cuisines from African to Vietnamese.

- **Crown Street, Surry Hills:** Eclectic mix with some of the best examples of modern Australian food, including bills 2 (9360 4762), MG Garage (9383 9383) and Prasit's Thai (9319 0748).

- **Cleveland Street, Surry Hills:** Lebanese eateries on the corner of Crown and Cleveland streets.

- **Chinatown:** Take your pick. BBQ King, 18 Goulburn Street (9267 2586) is basic but acclaimed by food critics for its perfect roast duck.

- **Norton Street, Leichhardt:** Little Italy in Sydney's inner west with pasta, gelato and coffee high on the menus.

- **Cockle Bay Wharf:** Sydney's first purpose-built restaurant complex, overlooking Darling Harbour, with everything from five-star Ampersand (9264 6666) to cafes and bars.

- **Crows Nest:** Northside shopping and restaurant centre. Sea Treasure (Chinese, 46 Willoughby Road, 9906 6388), Malabar (South Indian, 332 Pacific Highway, 9906 7343), and Bai Yok (Thai, 330 Pacific Highway, 9438 3941) are recommended.

FEAST OF SYDNEY

- An annual two-week food and wine festival in late June and early July showcasing the best in New South Wales fare. The festival, an initiative of Tourism New South Wales, features a variety of colourful events from the World's Longest Buffet at Darling Harbour to Eat Streets festivities, food and wine tours, and signature dishes at many of the city's leading restaurants; www.tourism.nsw.gov.au

General Information

BANKS
Bank trading hours are generally Monday to Thursday, 9.30am-4pm, Friday, 9.30am-5pm.
Major city banks open on weekdays at 8.30am. You'll need a passport or photo ID if cashing travellers' cheques.

CREDIT CARDS
All major credit cards (Visa, Mastercard, American Express, Diners Club) are accepted in most places and can be used to book and pay for hotel accommodation, restaurants, car hire, airline tickets, tours, concert and theatre tickets. You can also use most major credit cards to withdraw cash from automatic teller machines (ATMs).

ATMs
These can be found in the lobbies or external walls of many banks throughout the city. You can withdraw local currency directly from your own bank account with certain credit cards. You'll need your PIN number to access your account.

TRAVELLERS' CHEQUES
Larger stores will accept Australian dollar travellers' cheques issued by Thomas Cook and American Express (with passport ID) but you may have problems in smaller outlets. Foreign currency cheques should be cashed at banks, bureaux de change or your hotel.

DISABLED FACILITIES
Sydney has improved facilities for disabled people in recent years but there's still some way to go. Major city hotels, museums and attractions cater to the less mobile but you're advised to check in advance what facilities are available.

LIQUOR LAWS
Most licensed premises can sell alcohol from Monday to Saturday, 10am-10pm; Sunday hours vary. Restaurants, clubs and hotel lounges have more flexible hours. Many Sydney restaurants operate a BYO (bring your own) policy which means you can take your own wine. This can reduce the cost of your meal substantially, although there is a nominal charge for corkage. Some restaurants are licensed and BYO; check when booking.

POST OFFICES
Most post offices operate Monday to Friday, 9am-5pm. The General Post Office, 1 Martin Place, City (9244 3713), is open Monday to Friday, 8.15am-5.30pm, Saturday 10am-2pm.
Australia Post Customer Enquiries (131 317).

TELEPHONES
Most public payphones accept coins, credit cards and phone cards. Phone cards can be bought at newsagencies and Telstra outlets. Local calls are untimed and cost 50 cents.

INTERNET CAFES
There are several Internet cafes in Sydney. Check local telephone directories for addresses. Internet Cafe, Hotel Sweeney, cnr Druitt and Clarence streets (9261 5666), is centrally located.

TAXES AND TIPPING
Accommodation in city centre hotels is subject to a 10 per cent State Government bed tax. A national Goods and Services Tax (GST) will be fully operational by July 2000. Tipping is optional and not widespread; 10 to 15 per cent is customary in restaurants, either in cash or on your credit card. In taxis, a tip of $1 or $2 is acceptable for outstanding service.

MEDIA
Sydney has a fiercely competitive media. The major daily (Monday to Saturday) newspapers are The Sydney Morning Herald, The Daily Telegraph, The Australian and The Australian Financial Review. The Sunday newspapers are The Sun-Herald and The Sunday Telegraph. There are five TV networks: ABC (the national broadcaster), Channel 7, Channel 9 and Network Ten (commercial stations), and SBS (multi-cultural broadcaster), plus cable TV operators. There's also a variety of public and commercial radio networks, and local and international magazines.

Public Transport

FERRIES

- **Ferries and high-speed JetCats and RiverCats** operate from five wharfs at Circular Quay daily from 6.30am to midnight.
- **Sydney Ferries** operates nine routes to 35 harbour locations, and four daily harbour cruises, with Sydney Buses connecting with ferries at most wharfs. Private operators also offer ferry services from Circular Quay and Darling Harbour.
- **Tickets** (from $3.70 single) can be bought at wharf counters or automatic ticket machines. At larger wharfs, insert your ticket into an automatic barrier before boarding and on exiting. Tickets range from single-journey to the handy FerryTen, which allows 10 rides on inner harbour, Manly Ferry and JetCat, or Parramatta services. See Travel Passes (opposite) for combined ferry, bus and train tickets.

BUSES

- **Sydney's main bus terminals** are Circular Quay, Wynyard, Queen Victoria Building, Town Hall and Central.
- **The routes for Sydney Buses** are numbered:
  100-199 Manly and Northern Beaches
  200-299 Lower North Shore and Northern Suburbs
  300-399 Eastern Suburbs
  400-499 Inner Southern and Western Suburbs
  500-599 North Western and Upper North Shore
  600-699 Parramatta and Outer North-Western Suburbs
  700-799 Outer Western Suburbs
  800-899 South-Western Suburbs
  900-999 Southern Suburbs
  (buses 600 and upwards are private services).
- **Enter the bus** by the front door. Tickets (from $1.60 single) can be bought from the driver, so have small change ready. Keep your ticket until you get off the bus. If using a TravelTen, which allows 10 bus rides, insert it in the automatic machine on the bus on entry. See Travel Passes (opposite) for combined bus, train and ferry tickets.

> **Infoline:** (131 500) for Sydney Ferries, Sydney Buses and CityRail timetables and information, daily 6am to 10pm. Staff are on hand to advise on the best routes for your journey;
> www.sydneytransport.net.au

TRAINS

- **Suburban trains** run on 10 lines with Central Station as the main hub. Trains run daily between 4.30am and midnight (later on weekends).
- **A range of tickets** (from $2 single) are available from single-journey to all-day, weekly and longer-term tickets. You can buy tickets from station ticket offices or automatic machines. Display boards detail train routes.
- **Keep your ticket** for the duration of your journey. You have to insert it into an automatic ticket barrier to enter and exit platforms. The barrier will keep single tickets and return longer-term tickets for future use. See Travel Passes (opposite) for combined train, ferry and bus tickets.

TAXIS

- **Taxis can be hailed** on the street or at a cab rank; an illuminated roof light means they are available for hire. City centre ranks include Circular Quay, Wynyard, Town Hall and Central.
- **Taxi fares are metered**, with a $2 initial charge, and $2 toll if you cross the Harbour Bridge in either direction.
- **Not all Sydney taxi drivers speak English** or know where they are going. Check they understand your destination before you get in the cab. Many taxis accept credit cards; tipping is optional. Have small change ready for shorter journeys.
- **There is a changeover of taxi drivers** between 2.30pm and 3.30pm each day when cabs become scarce. You're advised to travel outside these times. See At a Glance section introductions for approximate taxi fares.
- **Call the Taxi Hotline** (1800 648 478) with complaints or compliments.

EXPLORER BUSES

Sydney Buses operates two sightseeing buses with commentaries.

- **The red Sydney Explorer** tours the city centre stopping at 24 of the most popular attractions. It departs Circular Quay daily every 17 minutes between 8.40am and 5.25pm. The last service returns at about 7pm.
- **The blue Bondi & Bay Explorer** makes 19 stops through the Eastern Suburbs, departing Circular Quay daily every 30 minutes between 9.15am and 4.20pm. The last service returns at about 6.15pm.
- **All-day tickets** on either service cost $28 adult and you are free to get on and off as you choose. Tickets can be bought from the driver.

MONORAIL

The above-ground monorail weaves through the heart of the city. It runs every three to five minutes daily 7am-10pm, Thursday to Saturday until midnight, and Sunday 8am-10pm.

- **Standard fare** is $3 adult, a Day Pass is $6. Fares are payable at each station kiosk.
- **There are seven monorail stations:** City Centre, Darling Park, Harbourside, Convention, Haymarket, World Square and Park Plaza. Maps are available at each station.

LIGHT RAIL

- **Metro Light Rail** is Sydney's newest transport system. It runs between Central Station and Wentworth Park, all day, every day, departing every eight to 15 minutes.
- **Fares** range between $2 and $4 with longer-term passes available. Fares can be paid to staff on the tram.
- **The stations** are Capitol Square, Haymarket, Exhibition Centre, Convention Centre, Pyrmont Bay, Star City, John Street Square and Sydney Fish Market.

SYDNEY AIRPORT

Sydney Airport (Kingsford Smith) is about nine kilometres from the city centre.

- **Bus and taxi ranks** are located outside the international and domestic terminals. A taxi ride to the city centre costs about $20. Expect long taxi queues in peak hours.
- **The green-and-yellow Airport Express** operates regular bus services between the airport and city centre (route 300), Kings Cross (350), Coogee and Bondi (351), and Darling Harbour and Glebe (352). You can pay the driver, $11 adult return (valid for two months).
- **Kingsford Smith Bus Service and Airport Clipper** operate between the airport and most city hotels. An underground rail link between the city and airport opens in early 2000.

TRAVEL PASSES

There are several "combined" public transport tickets which can reduce the cost of travelling around the city – ring (131 500) for full details – but two of the best are a TravelPass and SydneyPass.

- **A TravelPass** (from $26 weekly) includes unlimited seven-day travel on Sydney buses, trains and ferries (within certain zones).
- **A SydneyPass** includes return Airport Express journeys and three, five or seven days' unlimited travel on Sydney Explorer buses, regular buses, trains and all Sydney Ferries services. The pass costs $85, $115 and $135 adults respectively. Both passes are available from rail, bus or ferry ticket offices.

Useful Telephone Numbers

TOURIST INFORMATION
- **Sydney Visitor Centre**
  106 George Street, The Rocks, open daily 9am-6pm
  (9255 1788)
- **City information kiosks:**
  Circular Quay, Martin Place and George Street, next
  to the Sydney Town Hall
- **City Info Line** (9265 9007) Operates weekdays,
  9am-5pm providing What's On information
  www.cityofsydney.nsw.gov.au
- **NSW Travel Centre**
  International Arrivals Hall, Sydney Airport (9667 6050).
  If you want to know more about travel to Sydney or
  within NSW, contact the New South Wales Visitor
  Information Line (132 077) or access the Website at
  www.tourism.nsw.gov.au

EMERGENCY
- **Police, Fire, Ambulance**
  Dial 000 from any phone, 24 hours, free call.
  Police Switchboard (9281 0000)
- **City Police Stations**
  192 Day Street, City (9265 6499)
  132 George Street, The Rocks (9265 6366)
- **After Hours Pharmacy Information** (9235 0333)
- **Hotel Doctor**, 24 hours (9962 6000)
- **Sydney Hospital Emergency**
  Macquarie Street, City (9382 7111)

CITY CENTRE CHURCHES
- **Anglican:** St Andrew's Cathedral
  Sydney Square, George Street (9265 1661)
- **Catholic:** St Mary's Cathedral
  Cathedral Street (9220 0400)
- **Jewish:** The Great Synagogue
  166 Castlereagh Street (9267 2477)
- **Uniting:** St Stephen's Church
  197 Macquarie Street (9221 1688)
- **Interdenominational:** Wayside Chapel
  29 Hughes Street, Potts Point (9358 6577)

POSTAL SERVICES
- **General Post Office,** 1 Martin Place, City (9244 3713),
  open weekdays, 8.15am-5.30pm, Saturday 10am-2pm.
- **Australia Post Customer Enquiries** (131 317)

TELEPHONE SERVICES
- **Local Directory Inquiries** (013)
- **International Directory Inquiries** (1225)
- **Operator Assisted Calls** (1234)

CITY FOREIGN CURRENCY EXCHANGE
Any leading bank or:
- **American Express,** 92 Pitt Street (9239 0666)
- **Thomas Cook,** 175 Pitt Street (9231 2877)
- **Travelex,** 37-49 Pitt Street (9241 5722)
- **Interforex,** Wharf 6, Circular Quay (9247 2082)

LOST OR STOLEN CREDIT CARDS
- **Visa** (1800 805 341)
- **Mastercard** (1800 120 113)
- **American Express** (1800 230 100)
- **Bankcard** (9226 1122)
- **Diners** (1800 331 199)

SYDNEY AIRPORT
- **Administration** (9667 9111). Check with relevant
  airline for arrival/departure information
- **Qantas Domestic-International Reservations**
  (131 313)
- **Ansett Domestic Reservations** (131 300)
- **Ansett International Reservations** (131 414)

RAIL SERVICES
- **State Rail** switchboard (9219 8888)
- **CityRail Infoline**, daily 6am-10pm, (131 500)

WATER TAXIS
- **Harbour Taxis** (9555 1155)
- **Water Taxis** (9955 3222)

CAR HIRE
- **Avis** (136 333)
- **Budget** (132 727)
- **Hertz** (133 039)
- **Thrifty** (1300 367 227)

TAXI CABS
- **Legion Cabs** (131 451)
- **Premier Cabs** (131 017)
- **RSL Taxis** (132 211)
- **Taxis Combined** (9332 8888)
- **ABC** (132 522)

TICKET AGENCIES
- **Ticketmaster** (9320 9000)
- **Ticketek** (9266 4800)

For full details on the Sydney 2000 Olympic
Games, call (136 363) or visit the Olympic
Website at www.sydney.olympic.org

Index

Index

Index